Collaborating to
Meet Standards:

Teacher/Librarian

Partnerships

for 7–12

Toni Buzzeo
MA, MLIS

Linworth
PUBLISHING, INC

Published by Linworth Publishing, Inc.
480 East Wilson Bridge Road, Suite L
Worthington, Ohio 43085

ISBN 1-58683-024-4

5 4 3 2

Table of Contents

Collaborative Units

Index

Table of Figures

Politics and PowerPoint: *Bringing Julius Caesar into the 21st Century*

Recreating the American Civil War Era

Top 10 Lists for the Millennium

About the Author

About the Author

Toni Buzzeo is a practicing library media specialist at Longfellow Elementary School in Portland, Maine, as well as an author. She holds an M.A. from the University of Michigan in English Language and Literature and an M.L.I.S. from the University of Rhode Island. In 1999, she was named Maine Library Media Specialist of the Year by the Maine Association of School Libraries. As an educator, she has worked as a library media specialist for thirteen years and previously taught both high school and college English. As a writer, she is the author of professional books for librarians and teachers as well as two children's books. She is a frequent presenter at library, reading, and writing conferences. Her Web site, <www.tonibuzzeo.com>, offers additional insight into her many professional interests as well as her books. She can be reached at *tonibuzzeo@tonibuzzeo.com*.

Speaking Engagements

Librarians and educators who wish to contact Toni Buzzeo about conference and staff development speaking engagements related to Teacher-Librarian collaborations may visit her Web site at <www.tonibuzzeo.com>.

Acknowledgments

I want to thank my editor, Donna Miller, for her help and guidance. I also wish to thank my wonderful library media specialist contributors and their collaborative teaching partners for their generosity in sharing these collaborations, for countless hours of work in preparing their units for publication, and for having the good grace always to look for one more content standard, performance indicator, resource, or rubric to round out their contributions.

Dedication

To my library media specialist colleagues in the Portland Public Schools, Jo Coyne, Judy Wentzell, Louise Sullivan, Chris Bulsa-O'Meara, Carol Dunbar, Teri Caouette, Kelley McDaniel, Susie Knightly, Suzan Nelson, and Ellen McCarty, for your effort, your dedication, your willingness to share, and your collaborative efforts with teachers and within our small group of valiant souls.

Introduction

Since the publication of *Information Power: Building Partnerships for Learning* in 1998, we library media specialists have a "collaboration" mandate: "Collaboration for authentic, information-based learning—through shared planning, teaching, collection development, and management strategies—provides the model for all the program's connections to the larger learning community (AASL 123)." But, some wonder, is collaboration just the latest buzzword "consultation" once was? Is there likely to be a new word, a new mandate, just around the information literacy bend?

Buzz words. We all know them, speak them, write them, sometimes even resent them. A few years ago, in the Longfellow School Library Media Center in Portland, Maine, where I am Library Media Specialist, a colleague brand new to the staff interrupted a schoolwide curriculum development meeting to complain. "What does all that *mean*?" she demanded.

"All what?" we asked, stupefied.

"All that *jargon*."

Ahhh, I thought, the buzz words. Words such as learner expectations, content standards, key learnings, benchmarks, summative and formative assessment, and yes, **collaboration** were flying around the room. I wondered, is collaboration just another educational buzzword, or is it the clarion call in the wilderness of information literacy instruction?

Organizational "private-speak" can be a tool to improve communication on the inside but also to exclude those on the outside. Collaboration is a different sort of term. While it is a buzzword in educational circles, especially in library media specialist circles, it is also a word that carries the same meaning in the larger world: the world of politics, both national and international, the world of business, the world of community affairs, the world of family. At every level of human interaction, we collaborate for the benefit of all members of the group.

As a library media specialist with a career-long commitment to collaboration, it has always meant the opportunity to envision, plan, and teach in partnership with my colleagues, whether classroom teachers or other specialists, administrators, or public librarians, to meet the learning goals and standards identified for student achievement. Collaboration is a perfect means to address local, state, and national standards in education in order to achieve in student learning. In fact, collaboration has not only aided in achieving standards, but also in raising scores on standardized tests, another source of concern and occasional stress in the teaching profession. Standardized tests assess both declarative and procedural knowledge. In the library media center, we team with our colleagues to teach both content and process. Students, then, carry away not only content knowledge but also procedural knowledge and are able to apply their understanding to questions they encounter on local, state, and national assessments.

In recent years, as I attended countless collaboration workshops at countless library conferences (workshops stuffed to the hallways and spilling into them), it occurred to me that as a group, library media specialists were hungry for knowledge and assistance in collaborating. We wanted information. We wanted suggestions for overcoming roadblocks. We wanted practical, easily adoptable and adaptable units that worked!

And so the idea for this book was born. *Collaborating to Meet Standards: Teacher/Librarian Partnerships for 7–12* is written for practicing middle and high school library media specialists and their teaching partners. It is intended to be a guide in our endeavor to satisfy the 1998 *Information Power* mandate. First, the book includes a round-up of opinions, research, and philosophy from the library literature—and from working library media professionals—about collaboration. Also included are useful and practical suggestions for the implementation of collaboration and a discussion of its impact. Most important of all, however, the primary focus of this book is a collection of wonderful units written in a standardized template that you can borrow, adapt, and use in your own collaboration efforts.

You will find three, meaty introductory chapters. Chapter One is a history of cooperation and collaboration in school libraries over the past decade. Chapter Two examines the definitions and benefits (to administrators, to teachers, to library media specialists, and above all, to students) of collaboration and the studies that have proven its value, quantitatively. In Chapter Three, you will read about the factors necessary for success and the keys to overcoming roadblocks, including the stories of many practicing library media specialists who have struggled and succeeded with sticky scheduling problems, resistant teaching partners, and challenging school cultures. You will learn that, if necessary, you can even work with restrictions! And you will, I hope, become convinced that collaboration is not just a buzzword, but a goal worth striving for, a concept that offers benefits for library media specialists, teachers, students, and administrators. An index will allow you to search the concepts and ideas in these introductory chapters.

Following the introductory chapters, you will find a common template for use in planning collaborative units. It is clear, comprehensive, and easy to use. Finally, you will find a wealth of collaborative units contributed by library media specialist-and-teacher teams all over the United States. They are examples of best work, best thinking, best practice.

So step forward with me to the tune of the marching drum and heed the clarion call. Information literacy awaits!

Resources

American Association of School Librarians and Association for Educational Communication. *Information Power: Building Partnerships for Learning*. Chicago: American Library Association, 1998.

Collaboration: Where We've Been— Where We're Going

Setting the Stage

Picture this:

Date: May 2000
Cast: A class of high school juniors sporting laptops or PDAs, a physics teacher, a library media specialist
Scene: Redwood High School, Larkspur, California. Tables arranged in pods, some surrounded by computer systems in the reference room and some surrounded by books and magazines in the reading room. Glass door to computer lab open for easy access between areas. Media cart with laptop and data projector visible to class. Students sit in groups of five.

The teacher and library media specialist, who collaboratively designed the learning activity, review the prior class discussion, projecting class notes for easy reference. Groups report the sport they are researching, and the library media specialist leads a discussion on research strategies as he projects the school's online research handbook onto the screen. Students create concept maps while listening to the discussion.

After a brief and lively group consensus on individual roles and search options, groups scatter to gather data by linking to the science bookmarks, consulting the online periodical database, and searching science and sports encyclopedias. The library media specialist plays an archived copy of a videotape of soccer practice on a television preview monitor so students can analyze players' movements. He also provides a cable to download the critical points onto the iMac™.

During the following days, students work in the production area, pasting their scanned images and captions (with reference citations) onto posterboard. Other groups create *PowerPoint* presentations in order to capture the large file of animated screens and voice-over narration. Students move between project generation and research as they discover gaps in their knowledge. Both the library media specialist and the physics teacher coach students, check their progress, and lead a daily discussion on the process. A physical education teacher talks with students about their work and suggests that they share their projects with the sophomore fitness class or post them on the school's Web site.

At the end of the project, the library media specialist assesses the students' research process while the classroom teacher assesses the content and delivery. As they collaboratively analyze student work, they debrief their instruction and refine the project for next semester. The physics teacher has already recruited the biology teacher to craft a similar activity for their unit on human anatomy. (With thanks to Dr. Lesley S. J. Farmer for her contribution of this scenario)

Now turn the clock back nearly a century:

Date: 1904
Cast: A class of high school juniors, their English teacher, the school librarian, one of the first-appointed, professionally trained school librarians in the United States.
Scene: Library, Girl's High School, Brooklyn, New York. Long oak library tables, a Victrola on a corner table, leatherbound sets of poetry neatly lined up on mahogany shelves.

Unlike the collaborating library media specialist just described, whose job, as we know it, is defined by the criteria of expert teacher, instructional partner, information specialist, and program administrator, this librarian occupies the more traditional "keeper of the books" role.

She sits behind a circulation desk in a single reading room of approximately 3,000 volumes, lined up in perfect order. The English teacher leads his class through the door and nods cordially but cursorily at the librarian. His students follow him to the Victrola in the corner of the room. Seated at the long library tables, they listen to the recordings of English songs that the librarian has carried across the room to the teacher. At the teacher's prompting, students listen for elements the songs have in common with lyric poems they have been studying. Before the class leaves the library, the librarian removes the brand-new reference book, *The Columbia Grangers's Index to Poetry*, from the locked glass case where it is housed with other valuable reference books. She instructs the group in the use of the index then retreats to the circulation desk to check out student selections made from the leather bound sets of poetry by Keats, Wordsworth, and Shelley. As the class leaves the library, the English teacher once more nods at the librarian, this time a bit more graciously, and thanks her for her assistance. (Hall 627)

New Roles

By the mid-twentieth century, the role of the librarian as "keeper of the books" had begun to change. AASL standards published in 1960 and 1969 contributed to this change, and by 1975, the publication of the AASL standards, *Media Programs: District and School*, identified two instructional roles: design and consultation. (AASL 6) As a designer of instruction, the librarian was charged with initiating and participating in curriculum development. As a consultant, the librarian was to recommend media applications for instruction (Pickard n. pag.).

The Taxonomies

By 1982, the three elements of the library media program—traditional library services, audiovisual services, and instructional development—combined to create a new view of the role of the library media specialist (Loertscher, "The Second Revolution" 417). A variety of models for instructional development and design began to appear in the literature simultaneously with the first publication of Loertscher's library media specialist taxonomy in 1982. Collaboration had arrived on the school library horizon and has held sway in library literature ever since!

The 2000 revision of the taxonomy, published in *Taxonomies of the School Library Media Program*, 2nd edition, included ten levels of involvement.

The Library Media Specialist's Taxonomy
by David V. Loertscher

1. **NO INVOLVEMENT**
   The LMC is bypassed entirely.
2. **SMOOTHLY OPERATING INFORMATION INFRASTRUCTURE**
   Facilities, materials, networks, and information resources are available for the self-starter delivered to the point of need.
3. **INDIVIDUAL REFERENCE ASSISTANCE**
   The library media specialist serves as the human interface between information systems and the user.
4. **SPONTANEOUS INTERACTION AND GATHERING**
   Networks respond 24 hours a day and 7 days a week to patron requests, and the LMC facilities can be used by individuals and small groups with no advance notice.
5. **CURSORY PLANNING**
   There is informal and brief planning with teachers and students for LMC facilities or network usage—usually done through casual contact in the LMC, in the hall, in the teacher's lounge, in the lunch room, or by e-mail. [For example: Here's an idea for an activity/Web site/new materials to use. Have you seen…? There's a software upgrade on the network.]
6. **PLANNED GATHERING**
   Gathering of materials/access to important digital resources is done in advance of a class project upon teacher or student request.
7. **EVANGELISTIC OUTREACH/ADVOCACY**
   A concerted effort is made to promote the philosophy of the LMC program.
8. **IMPLEMENTATION OF THE FOUR MAJOR PROGRAMMATIC ELEMENTS OF THE LMC PROGRAM**
   The four LMC program elements—
      collaboration,
      reading literacy,
      enhancing learning through technology, and
      information literacy—
   are operational in the school. The LMC is on its way to achieving its goal of contributing to academic achievement.
9. **THE MATURE LMC PROGRAM**
   The LMC program reaches the needs of every student and teacher who will accept its offerings in each of the four programmatic elements.
10. **CURRICULUM DEVELOPMENT**
    Along with other educators, the library media specialist contributes to the planning and organization of what will actually be taught in the school or district (Loertscher 17).

In his February 1982 *Wilson Library Bulletin* article, "The Second Revolution: A Taxonomy for the 1980s," Loertscher emphasized the merits of each level; saying there was no need for guilt. He felt that the first necessary step was to accept the entire list as a collection of legitimate roles of instructional involvement, each level being "good" (417–418).

Yet, the higher one goes on the taxonomy, the more collaborative is the relationship between teacher and library media specialist. While the 1904 librarian profiled above might have hovered between Levels One and Four, it is Levels Eight through Ten that hint at and then extend the role of "instructional consultant" first introduced in the 1988 AASL *Information Power: Guidelines for School Library Media Programs* document (26). In other words, as Pickard pointed out in 1994, we were advised by our professional organization to stop being reactive, as described in Levels Three through Eight, and become proactive, as required by Levels Nine and Ten (n. pag.).

National Library Power Program

In 1988, through the National Library Power Program, the DeWitt Wallace-Reader's Digest Fund granted monies to New York City Public Schools to create library programs that improved the quality of education. By 1998, the program had been implemented at 19 sites (700 schools) nationwide serving more than one million children with an investment of more than $40 million. Collaborative planning was a major focus of Library Power professional development training sessions in both elementary and middle schools. In fact, the Library Power grant required that a site establish a totally flexible library program that employed collaborative planning. The fourth of six goals was to "Encourage collaboration among teachers, administrators, and librarians that results in significant improvement in the teaching and learning process."("National Library Power Program" n. pag.) Glenda Willnerd, Library Media Specialist, Lincoln High School, Lincoln, Nebraska reflects back on the experience and the long-term effects.

> Library Power provided us with funding to create a Lincoln Public Schools Guide to Integrated Information Literacy Skills or GIILS as we commonly called it. This guide was put together by a committee of library media specialists, technology liaisons, district consultants, and classroom teachers. The first edition was presented to all district staff through sessions presented by library media specialists and classroom teachers who did a lot of collaborating. The "Library Power Cadre" as they were called, modeled how to plan together and determine who was responsible for what part(s) of a lesson or unit, established a timeline, outlined expectations for students, and miscellaneous items such as graphic organizers and developing rubrics. All of these strategies were included in the GIILS guide. They also shared students' products, which was really bene-ficial for classroom teachers. (The revised guide includes information literacy skills for students in grades pre-K through grade twelve.) Now library media specialists and classroom teachers present the guide to new teachers in the dis-trict at their fall orientation. Teachers must attend a GIILS session before they can receive the guide (n. pag.).

According to Butt and Jameson, Library Power "became a formidable driving force for initiating and continuing support for professional collaboration between library media specialists and their classroom teachers" (n. pag.). Willnerd's experience proves that to be true.

Collaboration and Information Power

In a decade, the three roles of the library media specialist from *Information Power: Guidelines for School Library Media Programs* — information specialist, teacher, and instructional consultant (26) — had grown. By 1998, when *Information Power: Building Partnerships for Learning* was published, four roles were recommended — teacher, instructional partner, information specialist, and program administrator (4–5). The old "instructional consultant" role had been replaced with the updated term "instruction and curriculum partner." The "consultant" role of the 1988 document was outdated, inferring an unequal status, with the library media specialist more qualified than other teachers on the planning team (Muronaga and Harada 9). Partnership, on the other hand, implies equal status and participation. Diana G. Murphy, Head Librarian, The Kiski School, Saltsburg, Pennsylvania, explains the differences.

> I consider myself an instructional partner because it's my feeling that the classroom teacher, the library media specialist and the student are all partners in the learning process. The greatest learning will occur when there is cooperation, coordination, and collaboration. The consultant provides assistance when asked; the partner is an integral part of the total learning process (n. pag.).

Collaboration and Job Descriptions

State education departments and district central offices have taken up the charge in defining the teaching partner role of the library media specialist. In Wisconsin, the Department of Public Instruction, identifies content standards for initial and professional licensure of library media specialists. In both Communication and Group Dynamics, where the candidate can "Initiate and sustain collaborative instructional partnerships with teachers and other staff," and in Instructional Leadership, where the candidate can "Collaborate with teachers in teaching and evaluating instructional activities," there is a focus on the current collaborative role as defined by AASL ("Library Media Specialist Licenses" n. pag.). Likewise, West Hartford (Connecticut) Public Schools defines the role of the library media specialist in this way: "Library media specialists play an essential role in the learning community by collaborating with teachers, administrators and others to prepare students for the communication age" ("Library Media Services" n. pag.).

The New Frontier

Nor is it only library literature singing the praises of collaboration. Collaborative practice has become the focus of education at large. Teamwork for the purpose of improving instruction and student learning is being touted by top educational consultants and theorists. In 1998, when Assessment Experts Wiggins and McTighe set forth their "Understanding by Design" planning model in a book of the same title, they bemoaned lack of time for collaborative planning:

Historically, U.S. education has minimized the role of planning and design in teaching. The frenetic pace of daily school schedules, the demands of non-teaching duties, and the general lack of time reserved for planning (within and beyond the teaching day), make it difficult for educators to engage in substantive curricular planning and design work, especially with colleagues (158).

Furthermore, school improvement consultant Mike Schmoker devotes his entire first chapter of *Results: The Key to Continuous School Improvement* to 'Effective Teamwork,' designating collaboration as one of his three key components that favor results and improvement in schools. "We must acknowledge," he writes, "that schools would perform better if teachers worked in focused, supportive teams (10)." The focus, he says, must always be on student achievement. "Everyone in the educational community must work diligently to change the structures that impede teamwork. But meanwhile, we must take advantage of the opportunities that already present themselves—and which others have demonstrated can eventuate in better results (11)."

So, the age of collaboration has, indeed, arrived. We've experienced a change of enormous proportions throughout education and, in particular, in school librarianship—from the quieter, dustier turn of last century to these lively collaborative years of the new millennium. With our new mandate, vision, and skills, we're delving, alongside our teaching partners, into collaborative instructional design and delivery. This is clearly school librarianship's new frontier.

Resources

American Association of School Librarians and Association for Educational Communication. *Information Power: Building Partnerships for Learning*. Chicago: American Library Association, 1998.

American Association of School Librarians and Association for Educational Communication. *Information Power: Guidelines for School Library Media Programs*. Chicago: American Library Association, 1988.

American Association of School Librarians, American Library Association, and Association for Educational Communication. *Media Programs: District and School*. Chicago: American Library Association, 1975.

Butt, Rhonda and Christine Jameson. "Steps to Collaborative Teaching." Oregon School Library Information System. *OSLIS 2000 Implementation Manual*. 9 October 2000. 24 July 2002 <http://www.oslis.k12.or.us/develop/impman/>.

Hall, Mary E. "The Development of the Modern High School Library." *Library Journal* 40 (September 1915): 627.

"Library Media Services." *West Hartford Public Schools*. 24 July 2002 <http://www.whps.org/library/>.

"Library Media Specialist Licenses." *Wisconsin Department of Public Instruction; Instructional Media and Technology*. 24 July 2002 <http://www.dpi.state.wi.us/dltcl/imt/lmslic.html>.

Loertscher, David. "The Second Revolution: A Taxonomy for the 1980s." *Wilson Library Bulletin* 56 (February 1982): 417–421.

Loertscher, David V. *Taxonomies of the School Library Media Program*. 2nd ed. San Jose: Hi Willow Research & Publishing, 2000.

Muronaga, Karen, and Violet Harada. "The Art of Collaboration." *Teacher Librarian* 27:1 (October 1999): 9–14.

Murphy, Diana G. Personal interview. 12 February 2001.

"National Library Power Program." *American Library Association*. 4 August 1998. 24 July 2002 <http://www.ala.org/aasl/libpower/>.

Pickard, Patricia W. "Current Research: The Instructional Consultant Role of the School Library Media Specialist." *SLMQ* 21:2 (Winter 1993). 24 July 2002 <http://www.ala.org/aasl/SLMR/slmr_resources/select_pickard.html>.

Schmoker, Mike. *Results: The Key to Continuous School Improvement*. 2nd Edition. Alexandria, Virginia: Association for Supervision and Curriculum Development, 1999.

Wiggins, Grant and Jay McTighe. *Understanding by Design*. Alexandria, Virginia: Association for Supervision and Curriculum Development, 1998.

Willnerd, Glenda. Personal interview. 12 Feb. 2001.

Collaboration: How It Looks and Who It Benefits

Examining the Definitions

What IS collaborative planning? Recall the collaborative physics project from Chapter One, and we can draw some conclusions. Most importantly, collaborative planning is two or more equal partners who set out to create a unit of study based on content standards in one or more content areas plus information literacy standards, a unit that will be team-designed, team-taught and team-evaluated. Or, as the Nebraska Educational Media Association (NEMA) defines it, "Collaborative planning is teachers and library media specialists working together as an instructional team to plan for instruction that integrates information literacy skills and resources with curriculum objectives" ("Collaborative Planning" n. pag.).

There has been some confusion, since the 1980s, however, over the differences between three related concepts — cooperation, coordination, and collaboration. In *Collaboration*, a document in the AASL Learned Lessons series, Grover makes the point clearly. While in cooperation, the teacher and library media specialist work independently but come together briefly for mutual benefit, their relationship is loose. Coordination means there is a more formal working relationship and an understanding of shared missions. The teacher and library media specialist do some planning and communicate more. However, in collaboration, the two partners have a prolonged and interdependent relationship. They share goals, have carefully defined roles in the process, and plan much more comprehensively (Grover 2). Applying Loertscher's taxonomy, cooperation happens at Levels Three, Four, and Five; coordination happens at Levels Six and Seven; and collaboration begins with Level Eight, with full implementation at Level Nine (*Loertscher, Taxonomies of the School Library Media Program* 17).

Donham provides a comprehensive and visionary definition of that work at Level Ten:

> When teachers and library media specialists work together to identify what
> students need to know about accessing, evaluating, interpreting, and applying
> information; when they plan how and where these skills will be taught and how
> they relate to content area learning; when they co-teach so students learn the

skills at a time when they need them; and when they assess the students' process as they work with information as well as the end product, they have truly collaborated (21).

The library media specialist-teacher team is an educational gift. The library media specialist has familiarity with a broad range of resources as well as expertise in information skills and strategies, and the teacher has intimate knowledge of both the students and the content area. Pair them closely as equal partners from the inception of a unit through its execution and assessment, and the partners, the school community and the students are the lucky beneficiaries of the union.

Assessing the Benefits

So, what are the many benefits of the new collaborative model? Much attention has been justifiably afforded them in the professional literature. In *Collaboration*, Grover lists 10 global benefits of collaboration:

- Students are more involved in learning, and their work is more creative.
- Collaboration "ignites" creativity among teachers, and the "creative fire" spreads to learners.
- Modeling collaboration results in more collaboration among faculty in the school.
- Modeling collaboration influences students, teachers and parents, who learn to share ideas.
- Teachers, principals and librarians communicate more frequently.
- When students work in teams, the role of the teacher changes to that of resource person and learning facilitator.
- When students work in groups, the student's role changes also.
- Students learn to interact with people outside of the school.
- The library media program is integral to the collaborative teaching model.
- Administrators benefit professionally from their participation in teaching teams (Grover 7).

The Nebraska Education Media Association (NEMA), on the other hand, focuses more closely on the outcomes of collaborative planning. They assert that collaborative planning:

- promotes student achievement;
- promotes library media centers as central to the learning environment;
- promotes innovative instructional design;
- strengthens critical thinking and problem solving skills;
- provides opportunities for interaction between library media specialists and teachers;
- promotes sharing of resources;
- promotes integration and instruction of information literacy skills with the curriculum;
- enhances relevant use of all resources in all formats;
- provides opportunity for teachers to be aware of available resources;
- promotes intellectual freedom and equitable access to information and ideas;
- strengthens connections with the learning community ("Collaborative Planning" n. pag.).

Still another worthwhile view NEMA has taken of the advantages of collaboration is to look at the benefits to the various constituencies affected: administrators, library media specialists, teachers, and students.

Benefits to Administrators

Administrators benefit in a variety of ways from the collaborative planning of their teachers and library media specialists, as NEMA indicates. Beneficial instructional partnerships are developed, information skills, goals, and objectives are front and center and are integrated throughout the curriculum, the time and energy of the library media specialist is used effectively, and flexible scheduling is supported, providing time for teachers and library media specialists to plan together as well as ensuring that the library is utilized for comprehensive units addressing a variety of subject areas and content standards, often simultaneously. Most importantly, however, student achievement is improved. As Kent DeKoninck, Principal at Perry Meridian Middle School, Indianapolis, Indiana, notes, "Teacher-media specialist collaboration is essential to student achievement. The knowledge that media specialists possess provides an additional tool for teachers to facilitate a variety of enriched learning experiences" (n. pag.).

Benefits to Library Media Specialists

Of course, collaboration benefits library media specialists too. It allows us to use our wide-ranging skills in instructional design, teaching, assessment, information consulting, and program planning and administration. We have the chance to facilitate partnerships, integrate our information skills curriculum into content area instruction, promote the use of our many print and non-print resources, and develop a dynamic facility that serves as the instructional heart of the school. As a side benefit, Debra Kay Logan points out in her *Information Skills Toolkit*, collaboration leads students, teachers, and administrators to better understand the role, expertise, and responsibilities of the library media specialist (Logan 3). And, adds Willnerd, "I see the greatest benefit from collaborative planning as the opportunity to build relationships with teachers and other staff members and at the same time help students be successful as they research and learn" (n. pag.).

Benefits to Teachers

Teachers are also beneficiaries of the collaboration model. Through collaboration with the library media specialist, they have regular and practical opportunities to communicate their resource needs to the library media specialist, to practice resource-based instruction using a wide variety of resources, and to integrate information literacy into their content area instruction. In addition, partnering with the library media specialist lightens the load on the classroom teacher and makes teaching both more interesting and more effective. Renee Owens, English teacher at Hershey Middle School, Hershey, Pennsylvania, notes distinct benefits and advantages in collaborating with Librarian Penny Arnold. "Penny and I bounce ideas off one another, and usually what occurs is a bigger and better idea. Together we are better able to serve the students because we offer a variety in style, perspective, and expertise" (n. pag.). Cynthia Paul, Language Arts teacher at Kyrene Altadeña Middle School, Phoenix, Arizona, agrees. "As a classroom teacher who works with language arts students of all levels and abilities, I feel that my curriculum is very positively augmented by my collaboration with Media Specialist Nicki Hansen. I am able to maximize learning through the addition of multimedia projects that are facilitated by Mrs. Hansen and her knowledge of these library resources. I can't imagine teaching without her assistance" (n. pag.). Linda C. Thomas, media specialist, Barnard White Middle School, Union City, California, sums it up. "Through collaboration, teachers get non-stressful and non-evaluative partners to help them strengthen teaching skills and assessment" (n. pag.).

Benefits to Students

By far, the most important benefits of collaboration fall upon the students lucky enough to be taught by collaborating teachers and library media specialists. They learn independent use of relevant, integrated information skills, experience the excitement of resource-based learning, and have the advantage of at least two teachers for collaborative units. As Nancy Larimer, library media specialist, Lincoln Northeast High School, Lincoln, Nebraska, points out, "Students are the biggest benefactors of collaboration! When teachers and media specialists are able to create effective, efficient plans, students don't have to waste time. Clarification of expectations and objectives makes it easier for everyone" (n. pag.). Christopher J. Post, assistant headmaster, Kiski School, Saltsburg, Pennsylvania, concurs. In reflecting on Kiski as a "full laptop school" where every student and faculty member uses a laptop and every workspace is wired with high-speed Internet access, he notes, "Reading, writing, and thinking are augmented and facilitated with the use of technology, but there is no substitute for the process of good research. Our library staff, in collaboration with our faculty, ensure that our students continue to develop these skills and are prepared to use them as they move on to college and further in their professional careers" (n. pag.).

And it is, after all, student learning and student achievement that schools are all about! We collaborate, primarily, because as Donham asserts, we want learning to be meaningful, authentic, and applied (Donham 20). Assignments created by teachers and library media specialists in concert are more likely to be authentic, complex, and significant. Information skills are taught in context of new and creative units of study. As a result, students benefit and achievement rises.

Keith Curry Lance and Student Achievement Studies

The ongoing work of Keith Curry Lance, director of the Library Research Service, a unit of the Colorado State Library operated in partnership with the University of Denver's Library and Information Services Department, affords the most significant evidence of the positive impact of collaboration on students—the impact on student achievement. Lance's 1993 study, now referred to as the "First Colorado Study," was published as *The Impact of School Library Media Centers on Academic Achievement*. In addition to size of expenditure, staffing levels, and collection size as determinants of student performance, this landmark study revealed that students whose library media specialists played an instructional role tended to achieve higher average test scores (Lance 92–93). This finding led to further study with ever more significant results.

Lance's Alaska study, published in 2000 as *Information Empowered: The School Librarian as an Agent of Academic Achievement in Alaska Schools, Revised Edition*, also found an unequivocal link between school librarians and higher test scores—the more library staff, the greater the impact. In addition, this study also found that regardless of the level of librarian staffing, the more library media staff time devoted to delivering information literacy instruction, planning cooperatively with teachers, and providing in-service training to teachers and staff, the higher student test scores (Lance 65–66).

Pennsylvania determined in 1999 to be the first state east of the Mississippi to undertake a study of factors in school library media centers that impact student achievement. The study, published February 2000 as *Measuring Up to Standards: The Impact of School Libraries & Information Literacy in Pennsylvania Schools* showed a positive relationship between Pennsylvania System of School Assessment (PSSA) reading scores and library staffing. In addition, the report detailed, "as library staffing, information resources and information technology rise, so too does the involvement of school librarians in teaching students and teachers how to find and assess information" (Lance 6). Finally, the study found that test scores increase as school librarians spend more time, among other things, **teaching cooperatively with teachers**" (Lance 7).

The second Colorado study, published in 2000, *How School Librarians Help Kids Achieve Standards — The Second Colorado Study* carried the investigation even farther. It found that Colorado Student Assessment Program (CSAP) reading scores increased with increases in four library program traits. These include: program development, information technology, individual student visits to the library media center, and, most interestingly, **teacher/library media specialist collaboration**!

> A central finding of this study is the importance of a collaborative approach to information literacy. Test scores rise in both elementary and middle schools as library media specialists and teachers work together. In addition, scores also increase with the amount of time library media specialists spend as in-service trainers of other teachers, acquainting them with the rapidly changing world of information (Lance 7–8).

All this research adds up to new and indisputable knowledge: school library media specialists, particularly those working in collaboration with teachers as teaching partners, have an impact on student achievement. Furthermore, as Ken Haycock says, "Collaboration between teacher and teacher-librarian not only has a positive impact on student achievement but also leads to growth of relationships, growth of the environment and growth of persons" (Haycock 38). Collaboration is, then, a benefit to every member of the school community.

Resources

"Collaborative Planning: Partnerships between Teachers and Library Media Specialists." *NEMA — Nebraska Educational Media Association*. 24 July 2002 <http://nema.k12.ne.us/CheckIt/coplan.html>

DeKoninck, Kent. Personal interview. 8 April 2002.

Donham, Jean. "Collaboration in the Media Center: Building Partnerships for Learning." *NASSP Bulletin* 83:605 (March 1999): 20–26.

Grover, Robert. *Collaboration*. Chicago: American Association of School Librarians, 1996.

Haycock, Ken. "Collaborative Program Planning and Teaching." *Teacher Librarian* 27:1 (October 1999): 38.

Lance, Keith Curry, Christine Hamilton-Pennell, and Marcia J. Rodney. *Information Empowered; The School Librarian as an Agent of Academic Achievement in Alaska Schools, Revised Edition*. Juneau: Alaska State Library, 2000.

Lance, Keith Curry, Lynda Welborn, and Christine Hamilton-Pennell. *The Impact of School Library Media Centers on Academic Achievement*. San Jose: Hi Willow Research & Publishing, 1993.

Lance, Keith Curry, Marcia J. Rodney, and Christine Hamilton-Pennell. *How School Librarians Help Kids Achieve Standards: The Second Colorado Study*. San Jose: Hi Willow Research & Publishing, 2000.

Lance, Keith Curry, Marcia J. Rodney, and Christine Hamilton-Pennell. *Measuring Up to Standards: The Impact of School Libraries & Information Literacy in Pennsylvania Schools*. Greensburg, Pennsylvania: Pennsylvania Citizens for Better Libraries, 2000.

Larimer, Nancy. Personal interview. 12 Feb. 2001.

Loertscher, David V. *Taxonomies of the School Library Media Program*. 2nd ed. San Jose: Hi Willow Research & Publishing, 2000.

Logan, Debra Kay. *Information Skills Toolkit: Collaborative Integrated Instruction for the Middle Grades*. Worthington, Ohio: Linworth Publishing, Inc., 2000.

Owens, Renee. Personal interview. 8 April 2002.

Paul, Cynthia. Personal interview. 15 April 2002.

Post, Christopher J. Personal interview. 10 April 2002.

Thomas, Linda C. Personal interview. 11 Feb. 2001.

Willnerd, Glenda. Personal interview. 12 Feb. 2001.

Chapter Three

3

Collaboration: The Ideal and Its Many Variations

Factors for Success

What factors determine success in the effort to implement collaboration in library media centers? The library literature offers plenty of answers! For instance, the Nebraska Educational Media Association (NEMA) lists 15 "Elements for Successful Collaborative Planning" ("Collaborative Planning: How It's Done" n. pag.):

■ Administrative support
■ Shared philosophy, vision and goals
■ Flexibly scheduled library media center
■ Student centered teaching and learning
■ Shared decision making
■ Available resources and staffing
■ Professional partnerships and teaming
■ Effective communication
■ Respect
■ Good instructional design
■ Varied strategies for teaching and learning
■ Roles that are flexible yet identified
■ Staff Development
■ Time management
■ Education ("Collaborative Planning: How It's Done" n. pag.)

In *Collaboration*, Grover divides a similar list of 14 factors for success (which he terms "lessons") into six categories, Environmental Factors, Group Membership Characteristics, Process/Structure, Communication, Purpose, and Resources. However, it is his four lessons under "Environmental Factors" that will speak most meaningfully to individual school library media specialists adopting a collaborative model:

- Lesson 1. School culture must support collaboration.
- Lesson 2. Flexible scheduling is a vital component of collaborative planning and work.
- Lesson 3. The library media specialist can and should be a leader of the efforts to collaborate.
- Lesson 4. Expect apathy and/or dissent among faculty.

Add to that Lesson 9 under Process/Structure: "School administrators and other decision-makers must support the concept of collaboration (Grover 3-5)," and it's a pretty complete list of the essentials: school culture, favorable scheduling patterns, levels of trust and commitment in collegial relationships, and administrative support. Furthermore, Haycock notes that "the characteristics and actions of the people involved [are] most important" to collaborative planning (Haycock, "Collaborative Program Planning and Teaching." 38).

If Haycock is right, what strategies encourage positive characteristics and actions in the people involved? Berkowitz offers several suggestions to the library media specialist:

- Be prepared to offer suggestions for consideration.
- Share your concerns openly and honestly.
- Clarify roles and responsibilities.
- Focus on points held in common.
- Use humor.
- Provide open-ended suggestions.
- Be the "official" note taker and report back (n. pag.).

In addition, it is important to share common goals about what students will know and be able to do. Design-down instructional development models ensure that we begin with instructional goals, but in the absence of a design-down model, it is worth taking time to ensure that all members of the planning team agree on the desired student outcomes as well as the process.

Finally, much of the literature recommends the use of a planning form to ensure success. A form allows for efficient recording of goals, decisions, and responsibilities during planning sessions (recorded by the library media specialist, in Berkowitz's suggested "official" note taker capacity). The best planning forms are simple and straight-forward yet comprehensive enough to ensure that unit responsibilities, outcomes, and resources are clear and that the unit is easily replicable. The form on which the units in this book are recorded is one such template.

Overcoming Roadblocks to Success

The library literature reveals three major stumbling blocks: lack of administrative support, difficult scheduling patterns, and school culture/teacher resistance. One additional roadblock, lack of library media specialist interest, knowledge, or training, can also interfere. But we can often turn roadblocks around, work them to our advantage, and make them keys to success

The Role of the Administrator

As you read these three comments from practicing library media specialists, consider the ways that a principal can be a key to collaboration success. Mary Alice Anderson, media specialist, Winona Middle School, Winona, Minnesota, says:

My principal is very, very supportive. The way in which he helps the most is in giving me the freedom to do what needs to be done and encouraging teachers to use technology and resources, to try different things. He never stands in the way of innovation. He wants the kids to have positive experiences in the media center (4 Dec. 2001, n. pag.).

And Murphy's experience is the same. "Our headmaster has been totally supportive. Although he is from the old school, he seems to have complete faith in my abilities and supports any initiative I pursue" (4 Dec. 2001, n. pag.). In addition, Murphy's headmaster provides support by providing time. "There are several unassigned periods of time for faculty to meet with the LMS or other teachers, including two coffee meetings a day (10:30 a.m. and 7:00 p.m.) in his house" (4 Dec. 2001, n. pag.). Penny Arnold, librarian, Hershey Middle School, Hershey, Pennsylvania, adds that her principal also provides support for collaboration by ensuring "time in the beginning of the year, time with new teachers, time during faculty meetings, and time to meet with teams during team time. I have a flexible schedule and planned times to meet with teams each month and on an as-needed basis. My principal would also allow a professional day for large unit planning" (5 Dec. 2001, n. pag.). The first two administrators provide strong support for collaboration primarily by supporting the library media specialists in their efforts, offering them freedom to innovate and to launch new initiatives. The second and third also recognize the essential nature of time as a support.

According to Haycock, research findings show that "Collaborative planning requires a knowledgeable and flexible teacher-librarian, with good interpersonal skills and a commitment to integrated information literacy instruction, and **the active support of the principal**" (Haycock, "Collaborative Program Planning and Teaching" 38). In fact, he says, "The role of the principal is so critical to the development of school priorities, culture, and resources that it would be fair to say the principal is the key factor in developing an effective and integrated school library program" (Haycock, "Collaborative Program Planning and Teaching" 38).

What, then, are the ways a principal who understands the value of the collaborative model supports it? Chief among them are expectations. Van Deusen's 1993–94 AASL/Highsmith Research Award Study revealed that curriculum consultation was significantly higher when the principal expected teacher-librarian collaborative planning (Van Deusen n. pag.). This, of course, demands an administrator who is willing to offer strong leadership and take risks. He or she must be willing to design job descriptions, hire new teachers, and set goals with current faculty with explicit expectations for collaboration. "When an administrator asks classroom teachers how they are using the media center resources and the expertise of the teacher-librarian, the probability of collaboration between the teacher-librarian and classroom teachers is likely to increase" (Bishop and Larimer 20). In addition, principals can include collaboration expectations in evaluations, observe planning sessions between teachers and library media specialists, monitor and log collaboration events, and provide in-service instruction in collaboration (Donham 24).

But what can we do to enlist the support of the principal concerning collaboration? There are a multitude of ways, large and small, to encourage him or her. First, say secondary library media specialists, find out what's important to your administrator and play to it. Gail Barraco, director, Broome Tioga School Library System, Broome Tioga BOCES, Binghamton, New York, says, "I think the idea is to show your value by finding out what is important to them and addressing it. Do something your administrator needs done." She reflects back on her days as a building specialist. "I e-mailed the White House during the Clinton administration for my principal to see if they could send a birthday greeting to his mother who was going to be celebrating her eightieth birthday. She was sent a greeting signed by the President" (10 Feb. 2002 n. pag.). Maureen Irwin, library director, Rye Country Day School, Rye, New York, concurs. "I think it's important to know your principal's 'weak spots' — the things he considers really important, and address those" (10 Feb. 2002 n. pag). And remember, those 'weak spots' may be personal or they may be professional.

The second approach is to gain the administrator's support and make him or her look good. Murphy explains.

> First, and most importantly, the LMS must gain the respect and trust of the principal. At the first faculty meeting of the new school year (when I started in my current position) I asked to speak to the group. I emphasized the services available to the teachers from the Library Media Center. After the meeting, the Headmaster who hired me took me aside and said, 'Thanks! You made me look good.' That initial request to speak to the group paved the way for further cooperation with the administration and the faculty. It was then a few short steps to develop coordination and then collaboration (11 Feb. 2002 n. pag.).

Third, we must be our own best advertisers. Don't JUST collaborate. Toot your horn. Anderson certainly recommends this course. She advises, "Share new ideas with teachers; when they are successful tell the principal what you did to introduce the idea to the teacher" (10 Feb. 2002 n. pag.) and offers an example of her success in doing just that.

> For example, I recently introduced the software Inspiration to a 6th teacher whose students are studying the 'Five themes of geography.' She was very excited about it; I introduced it to the students and she said it would be an option for them to use it to complete their project. The kids are enthused and doing well; next year it will be a requirement to use Inspiration. When I place the order for more copies of the software I will explain my role and how it is leading to student enthusiasm and success. I think it's important to describe our role in terms of student and teacher success (10 Feb. 2002 n. pag.).

Lynn Rutan, Librarian, Macatawa Bay School, Holland, Michigan, concurs. "We continually 'talk up' collaboration. I think it is really important to keep it out front with both teachers and administrators. They need to be reminded of the effort and the excellent results" (n. pag.).

Fourth, Dr. Lesley S. J. Farmer, formerly library media teacher, Redwood High School, Larkspur, California, and currently associate professor at California State University Long Beach, suggests appealing to the administrator's competitive spirit. She believes that targeting the administrator's healthy competition and sense of equity will help you achieve your goal. "If neighboring schools have good collaborative models, showcase them to your administrator. Arrange to have your principal see a model school in action, live or on video, or get a principal from a model school to invite your principal to his or her school" (11 Feb. 2002 n. pag.).

Fifth, in order for you to achieve success in overcoming administrative roadblocks, the principal must be informed about collaborative planning and library media center usage through regular communication. In turn, the library media specialist must keep the principal informed by sharing the weekly schedule, preparing monthly reports, and inviting the observations of or participation in library media center learning activities. We must play our role in this communication process if we expect to garner the administrative support that collaboration requires. To extend the communication/advertising theme, Leslie Preddy, media specialist, Perry Meridian Middle School, Indianapolis, Indiana, suggests a collaboration log.

> I have gained a great deal of support from my principal through maintaining a collaboration log. Each entry on the log begins with a collaborative planning worksheet that I fill out and I attach to that worksheet copies of e-mails, rubrics, information literacy skills mini-lessons, etc. I turn the log in to my principal at the end of every month. He reviews it and usually has a few insightful comments for me when he returns it to me. I receive more understanding and support from administration since I began this procedure than ever before — and it's a wonderful feeling to know that, without taking too much of my principal's time, he's learning to understand more of what I do (11 Feb. 2002 n. pag.).

Finally, read Section 8, "Start with the Building Principal" in Gary N. Hartzell's thought-provoking book, *Building Influence for the School Librarian*. Not only will you find practical suggestions for changing your relationship with your administrator, but throughout the book, you'll have opportunities to think about yourself, your job, your role in the school, and your ability to shape and influence each of those things. Murphy says, "I believe that 'building influence' is the key to success for the LMS." In fact, she says, "During this past school year, PSLA (Pennsylvania School Librarians Association) did regional workshops entitled: 'Tapping Your Influential Potential: Building Influence with Teachers and Administrators' based, in part, on the Hartzell book" (11 Feb. 2002). This PSLA presentation is available at <http://www.psla.org/pslaworkshops/fall2001.doc> for educational, nonprofit use.

It all takes time, patience, and hard work, of course. But the long term goal, overcoming roadblocks to success with your administrator, make it worth the effort.

Time and Scheduling

The issues of time and scheduling are the next potential set of roadblocks to be overcome. The first hurdle is sometimes scheduling. While it is not the endemic roadblock that it often is in elementary schools, many of which still follow a rigid schedule of classes in the library media center, secondary scheduling patterns can present their own challenges! Barraco looks back at her experiences as a building library media specialist. "There was no block scheduling at the school where I taught. The confines of the school day and the new Regents requirements made what little free time there was, extinct. Now those periods were taken up by alternative intervention services (remediation)" (4 Dec. 2001 n. pag.). Willnerd adds, "We have an eight period day, and with a school of this size (2,200 students in grades 10 to 12), scheduling becomes a problem" (n. pag.).

On the other hand, many secondary library media specialists find that both the traditional schedule and newer block schedules are working well to provide collaboration opportunities. Larimer reports, "We have traditional scheduling, which includes two planning periods a day for all teachers. Scheduling isn't a roadblock in our situation" (4 Dec. 2001, n. pag.). And Anderson adds, "We have a modified block schedule; it is fantastic. We have two teams for each grade level so it's very easy to know which team is doing what and ensure equity" (4 Dec 2001, n. pag.). Finally, Jo Ann Wahrman, Librarian, Goodland High School, Goodland, Kansas, has a full block schedule and is equally pleased. "We have a block schedule, and it lends itself to collaboration. Teachers feel they have time to work with the library" (n. pag.).

The second, larger roadblock to collaboration in the secondary school, however, is often a lack of time. For Willnerd, it is the demands on her own time that sometimes get in the way. "Yes, time is a potential roadblock to collaborative success because we have so many classes in the media center, it is difficult to find a block of time to sit down and plan with teachers" (n. pag.). For Irwin, it's also a matter of limitations on teacher time. "Teachers feel pressured to include so much content they are reluctant to 'give up' a class to instruction in research skills" (n. pag.). Anderson agrees. "Teachers are swamped. We don't fit the textbook model of collaboration but instead work in bits and pieces" (4 Dec. 2001, n. pag).

Realistically, you are less likely to be able to influence the schedule as a whole than how staff use it, or work within it. As always, communication is the key. One possibility is to create a school library committee composed of teachers and students to brainstorm solutions to scheduling roadblocks and time constraints in order to more effectively meet student learning needs. Second, the creation of a 'position paper' (including Background, Current Situation/Problem, Options for Solution of the Problem, and Recommended Course of Action) might be a starting point for presenting concerns to administrators. Once you've written the paper, make an appointment to meet with your principal to present its contents and discuss your proposed course of action. Third, join forces with teachers whom the principal respects and with whom you have a successful collaborative relationship. Finally, simply be visible with your program, both for the sake of influencing administrative opinion and to help teachers see the value of using precious time to plan with you. Barraco suggests:

> Send out a newsletter marketing your services, whether it's print, e-mail, or a link you've pushed from your page. Market those services aggressively, letting teachers know that you are accessible and value collaboration. Provide them with research about the benefits of a flexible schedule in being able to get to teachers. Cite the Lance studies that make the connection between higher academic achievement and quality school library media programs (11 Feb. 2002 n. pag.).

Can you overcome the huge roadblock of time, then? The final solution points back to the administrator, of course. However, the task requires creativity by administrators, librarians, and teachers all of whom value collaboration. And let's face it, sometimes it's just a matter of coming in early or staying late to meet and take the most important first step—planning.

School Culture

The third potential roadblock to teacher-library media specialist collaboration is school culture. When a school lacks a collaborative work culture, teaching partnerships and collaboration have nothing on which to build. Consider Farwell's formula for successful collaboration. "The most promising formula for successful information literacy instruction is a combination of an energetic, knowledgeable, open-minded, and committed library media specialist; a flexible, confident, team-oriented staff; a risk-taking principal who understands change, how to manage both people and budgets, and the advantages and needs of an integrated resource-based instructional program; and a system for providing regular, collaborative planning time during the school day" (Farwell 30). Administrators, teachers, and library media specialists all must see collaboration as an effort worth a risk. The value of a collaborative climate in the school, then, cannot be underestimated!

Many secondary library media specialists report that a collaborative school culture is more likely to exist in middle schools than in high schools. Larimer reflects on this situation,

> The high school classroom teacher considers him/herself the specialist in the specific field of study. It seems to be very difficult for him or her to give up any part of the classroom domain. Many do not see the media specialist as a teacher. Therefore, collaboration overall is very difficult for many high school teachers. When I was a middle school LMS, there was far more collaboration. High school teachers still often think of the media center only when they want to do the traditional 5- to 10-page research paper (4 Dec. 2001, n. pag.).

Anderson agrees. "That is a major issue. I've been very successful at my middle school, but senior high schools tend to have a departmental, isolationist culture. Studies show that change happens slowly at senior high" (4 Dec. 2001, n. pag.). And yet, library media specialists at both middle and high school report great success in collaborating with colleagues. An enthusiastic, hard-working, and collegial librarian can make it happen!

Barraco, in her role as district Director, Media Library Services, referring to the need to be proactive, says,

> Old ways die hard and the perception of the library media center and the library media specialist is something that needs to be constantly addressed. If a school has a traditional perception of what a library is and what a librarian does, it may not reflect the reality of libraries today. Why and how? Public relations with staff is essential and working with them in their committees and interest groups is very important. Librarians need to address what their teachers, administrators and students need and infuse themselves in the process. They will never achieve success in their programs if they expect everyone to come to them. That just doesn't work. Building trust goes a long way toward encouraging further collaboration (4 Dec. 2001 n. pag.).

In their article, "The Art of Collaboration," Muronaga and Harada agree. They begin by suggesting that the library media specialist must be willing to lead or to be an active team member as the situation requires (10). They outline eight steps to developing a collaborative culture: building trust, developing collaborative relations, creating leadership teams, planning interactive meetings, valuing strengths, varying roles and responsibilities, emphasizing team work, and viewing planning as a nonlinear, holistic, and dynamic process. (10-14). Many of the contributors to this book share Muronaga and Harada's beliefs and experiences.

Farmer believes in building trust with a teaching staff. She suggest that library media specialists "overcome resistance through communication, get to know people better, do good work and build a good reputation, and practice patience and responsiveness" (12 Feb. 2001, n. pag.). As Farmer points out, patience is important to developing collaborative relations over time. That has certainly been Anderson's experience.

> Some teachers want to work alone and it is best to respect their wishes and trust that for the time being, their students will meet with success without our input. Eventually, most people do seek out help and advice; that is the time to "jump in." I also know that the entire idea of collaboration is foreign to teachers so we

can't be pushy. We can encourage, offer to help, and do a good job when we do work with people (n. pag.).

Larimer agrees. "The biggest roadblock at the high school level is lack of experience in collaboration. It's difficult to break through the old barriers of each teacher being a specialist in his field, not accustomed to someone else wanting to assist in their planning. However, once I've had success with someone, they often come back for more" (4 Dec. 2001, n. pag.).

Another useful enterprise is the creation of and participation in leadership teams. If the library media specialist steps forward when there are building or district initiatives, he or she will have an opportunity not only to participate but also to collaborate. Ann Marie Pipkin, media specialist, Hoover High School, Hoover, Alabama, believes this is true. "We are encouraged in IP2 to take a leadership role in our school, and by doing so, as a member of the technology and professional development committees, I feel this opens the door to collaboration." She goes on to describe her specific success in this arena.

> I strongly believe that by being a member of my technology committee and presenting schoolwide workshops on electronic resources and search strategies, my colleagues feel more comfortable collaborating with me in instances where they want to integrate technology into their lesson and do not feel that they have the expertise. With two 24-computer research labs in the media center directly under my control and supervision, teachers know that technology as well as print resources can be incorporated easily and successfully into their lessons (12 Dec. 2001, n. pg.).

In planning interactive meetings, librarians wishing to collaborate must allow for a variety of venues and be flexible says Arnold. "Being in the middle school with a flexible schedule has afforded the opportunity to meet and plan with teachers many times. I try to meet with teams one time per month to share new resources (books, magazines, Web sites, etc.) and discuss any planned units. Training is ongoing in all of the library's technology and also occurs during those meetings" (12 Feb. 2001, n. pag.). And think about your own varied times and venues, between classes, in the halls, over lunch—any place and time available to grab a second and a word.

Valuing strengths and acknowledging individual differences in our teaching partners is also important. Pipkin, says, "I have seen teachers willing to collaborate who don't know where to begin. It helps to take them along very slowly. They then come back again better prepared and more in control of what they actually want to do. You just cannot ask too many questions too quickly. Slow and easy make them repeat collaborators" (10 Dec. 2001, n. pag.). Anderson advises, "Work with the living—work with those who want to do things differently. Success breeds success" (12 Feb. 2001, n. pag.).

Simultaneously, it is important to be sensitive to the need for varying roles and responsibilities in collaborative partnerships. Pipkin says she is alternately a consultant and a collaborative partner, depending on the attitude of the teacher. "I offer my services and many times work with the teacher as a partner, but more often as a consultant" (12 Feb. 2001, n. pag.). Perhaps the underlying necessity in a collaborative school culture is an emphasis on teamwork. The library media specialist can become the cheerleader for team members' assumption of a variety of roles and responsibilities in the planning and execution of collaborative units.

Finally, it is important to remember that the planning process and the development of collaborative partnerships do not always proceed in a lockstep, linear fashion. Sometimes, we have to come in through the back door with patience and a plan. Preddy relates her experience.

> The most successful collaborations I have participated in have been when I have been able to get to know a teacher well enough to find out where his/her main interests lie. Once I have that, I begin to share resources that I think might interest him or her and build from there (idea sharing, creative funding, etc). Once there is evidence that I care about what interests the teacher and have resources and ideas to support that interest, the collaboration is easy (12 Feb. 2001, n. pag.).

Working with Restrictions

But what if you have done all you can by way of developing a collaborative culture and there are still roadblocks ahead of you? How do you work with restrictions and still move forward? Establishing collaboration takes time. Haycock claims, "Changes as complex as collaborative program planning and team teaching that reflect different approaches to teaching and learning do not take place quickly or easily; they are evolutionary, usually over two to five years . . ." (Haycock, "Fostering Collaboration, Leadership and Information Literacy" 83). What, then, to do in the two to five years of change? How do you use those years to your best advantage?

First, remember that trust is the bedrock of collaboration. As Pipkin notes, "The level of trust the students have is in direct proportion to the trust that the teachers have in me. The students can sense that" (12 Feb. 2001, n. pag.). The more trust you can engender in the teachers you hope to collaborate with, the more likely they are to meet you half way. Here's how Preddy proceeds.

> Once I've collaborated with a teacher, team taught once, he or she comes back again and again. But the resistance to it initially is pretty strong. Some say that it is because they feel I am too busy, but more often than naught, I think it has more to do with me taking the time to be pro-active. I have to go out in the building and touch base with people, find out what they're doing, offer ways that I can help. Otherwise, I end up getting the "warehouse" approach to the library media center, where classes come in at the last minute for some haphazard research planned in isolation by the classroom teacher (10 Dec. 2001, n. pag.).

Building trust is an important first step, even when the path seems completely blocked.

Second, assess the comfort level of various teachers and match the collaborative activity you suggest with that comfort level. Murphy's experience is a good example. "Coming on strong never works for me," she says. "Subtlety works better. If I can't get a teacher to bring classes to the library, I go to them" (10 Dec. 2001, n. pag.). She explains,

> Last year during a poetry unit, I went to a resistant teacher and volunteered to read my favorite poems to her classes. She agreed and as a follow up to my day

with her classes, she invited the entire faculty to come to read to her classes. About 10 teachers volunteered. She then brought her classes to the library and we offered biographical info for authors involved and assistance in compiling poetry booklets with the students. The teacher is now hooked. She began this year with a great collaborative mythology unit, and we have already planned an exciting project for Black History Month (10 Dec. 2001, n. pag.).

Anderson adds, "It's important to always consider personalities and extenuating circumstances. It's important to do a good job when you do work with people—bend over backwards to help them if need be" (12 Feb. 2001, n. pag.). It's one more inroad to collaborative success.

Which leads me to a theory shared with me by my principal, Sheila Guiney, at the start of my first professional school library job, at Margaret Chase Smith School in Sanford, Maine. I was discussing the need to bring all staff members on board with flexible scheduling and collaboration. She told me that she'd been in a workshop many years before in which she'd learned a theory that applied to every situation in which a group of people are asked to change. In every group, she said, there will be three clusters, divided roughly into thirds. The first cluster is the "Oh yeah's!" These folks will instantly come on board for a change that they see as exciting, beneficial, and inspiring. The second cluster, she said, is the "Yeah, but's." This group watches and waits while the "Oh yeah's" jump on board and take the change for a test drive. After the change proves worthy, usually once a full year has gone by, they're willing to hop up to the wheel. Last are the "No way in heck's." This cluster holds stubbornly to the old ways. Even in the light of success experienced by the first two groups, they will not change until forced to change. That's where a risk-taking, forward-seeing administrator proves a wonderful ally.

Several of the contributors to this book have shared that same experience and recommend using this knowledge to your benefit. Anderson says,

> I think teachers start to work with you when they see other teachers doing interesting things with media/technology or hear kids talking about it. It's important to reach out to those who like to move forward and try new approaches to teaching. It's also important to build on small successes. We reach teachers through good service and assistance when they need it. After time, we learn whom we can reach out to, when we can reach out to them, and how (9 Dec. 2001, n. pag.).

Farmer adds her own list of recommendations.

- Go for the early adopters, and build on success.
- Let the positive grapevine work.
- Let satisfied customers be your intro to the associated department or grade.
- Work through the kids.
- Keep plugging.
- Be patient.
- Model best practice.
- Explain your position.
- Talk in teacher terms—reach out (9 Dec. 2001, n. pag.).

Finally, she says, "It's better to be responsive (the golden learning moment when folks ask for your help) than to be pro-active when they're not ready" (9 Dec. 2001, n. pag.). Arnold has succeeded on the path in just this way. "Collaboration efforts in my current job were won one by one — as each teacher saw success and excitement in lessons in both the kids and other teachers. I am now dealing with — and this the norm — 35 scheduled classes next week, varying only between 6th and 8th grade this week, and the topics range from author studies, individual research projects, to space, and Canada" (9 Dec. 2001, n. pag.). I think we'd all agree that Arnold's is a success story!

What are the keys then? First, respect individual strengths. Form alliances with the collaborative superstars, the "Oh yeah's." Create initial successes with them. Advertise these successes. Build on them. Remain flexible. Don't expect everyone to participate at the same level. Learn to compromise for the sake of forward momentum. Last of all, remember: word of mouth is the best ally you have. Spread the word. And, above all, keep the faith!

Resources

Anderson, Mary Alice. Personal interview. 12 Feb. 2001.

Anderson, Mary Alice. Personal interview. 4 Dec. 2001.

Anderson, Mary Alice. Personal interview. 9 Dec. 2001.

Anderson, Mary Alice. Personal interview. 10 Feb. 2002.

Arnold, Penny. Personal interview. 12 Feb. 2001.

Arnold, Penny. Personal interview. 5 Dec. 2001.

Barraco, Gail. Personal interview. 4 Dec. 2001.

Barraco, Gail. Personal interview. 10 Feb. 2002.

Berkowitz, Robert E. "TIPS (Teaching Information Problem-Solving): Collaboration for Success." *The Big6 Teaching Technology & Information Skills eNewsletter*. E-1:2 (Spring 2000). 24 July 2002 <http://www.big6.com/enewsletter/archives/spring00/tips.html>.

Bishop, Kay and Nancy Larimer. "Literacy through Collaboration." *Teacher Librarian* 27:1 (October 1999): 15–20.

"Collaborative Planning: How It's Done." *NEMA — Nebraska Educational Media Association*. 24 July 2002 <http://nema.k12.ne.us/CheckIt/model.html>.

Donham, Jean. "Collaboration in the Media Center: Building Partnerships for Learning." *NASSP Bulletin* 83:605 (March 1999): 20–26.

Farmer, Dr. Lesley S. J. Personal interview. 12 Feb. 2001.

Farmer, Dr. Lesley S. J. Personal interview. 9 Dec. 2001.

Farmer, Dr. Lesley S. J. Personal interview. 11 Feb. 2002.

Farwell, Sybil. "Successful Models for Collaborative Planning." *Knowledge Quest* 26:2 (January/February 1998): 24-30.

Grover, Robert. *Collaboration*. Chicago: American Association of School Librarians, 1996.

Hartzell, Gary N. *Building Influence for the School Librarian*. Worthington, Ohio: Linworth, 1994.

Haycock, Ken. "Collaborative Program Planning and Teaching." *Teacher Librarian* 27:1 (October 1999): 38.

Haycock, Ken. "Fostering Collaboration, Leadership and Information Literacy: Common Behaviors of Uncommon Principals and Faculties." *NASSP Bulletin* 83:805 (March 1999): 82–87.

Irwin, Maureen. Personal interview. 4 Dec. 2001.

Irwin, Maureen. Personal interview. 10 Feb. 2002.

Larimer, Nancy. Personal interview. 12 Feb. 2001.

Larimer, Nancy. Personal interview. 4 Dec. 2001.

Muronaga, Karen and Violet Harada. "The Art of Collaboration." *Teacher Librarian* 27:1 (October 1999): 9–14.

Murphy, Diana G. Personal interview. 4 Dec. 2001.

Murphy, Diana G. Personal interview. 10 Dec. 2001.

Murphy, Diana G. Personal interview. 11 Feb. 2002.

"Pennsylvania School Librarians Association Fall 2001 Professional Development Workshop." *Pennsylvania School Librarians Association*. 24 July 2002 <http://www.psla.org/pslaworkshops/fall2001.doc>.

Pipkin, Ann Marie. Personal interview. 12 Feb. 2001.

Pipkin, Ann Marie. Personal interview. 10 Dec. 2001.

Pipkin, Ann Marie. Personal interview. 12 Dec. 2001.

Preddy, Leslie. Personal interview. 12 Feb. 2001.

Preddy, Leslie. Personal interview. 10 Dec. 2001.

Preddy, Leslie. Personal interview. 11 Feb. 2002.

Rutan, Lynn. Personal interview. 11 Feb. 2002.

Van Deusen, Jean Donham and Julie I. Tallman. "The Impact of Scheduling on Curriculum Consultation and Information Skills Instruction: Part One, The 1993–94 AASL/Highsmith Research Award Study." *School Library Media Quarterly* 23:1 (Fall 1994): 17–25.

Wahrman, Jo Ann. Personal Interview. 4 Dec. 2001.

Willnerd, Glenda. Personal interview. 5 Dec. 2001.

Using the Template

Elements of the Template

The template used in this book was designed after poring over numerous templates from professional resources and colleagues, and examining many more from contributors. The best elements from each source were borrowed and then several contributors were asked to "test drive" the result. All found this template to be both comprehensive and user friendly and hopefully, you will too. The elements are as follows:

Header: Includes Unit Title, Library Media Specialist Name and Title, Teacher Name(s) and Title, School Name, School Address, School Phone Number, and Library Media Specialist E-mail Address

Grade Level: Grade(s) that has/have participated in this unit.

Unit Overview: Description of the unit of study, focusing on goals, student learning, and student activity.

Time Frame: From start to finish, the unit takes this time to complete.

Content Area Standards: Exclusive of Information Skills Standards (listed below), content area(s) and standards targeted for each, drawn from local, state, or national guidelines.

Information Power Information Literacy Standards and Indicators: Drawn from IP Literacy Standards document in *Information Power: Building Partnerships for Learning.* (AASL 1998). Information Literacy Standards are reproduced, with permission, here. To view the indicators, AASL invites you to read *Information Power: Building Partnerships for Learning.*

Cooperative Teaching Plan: Major teaching responsibilities of the library media specialist and teaching partner(s) for this unit.

Library Media Specialist Will:

Teacher(s) Will:

Resources: A list of outstanding resources for use in the unit and a summary of other helpful sources.

Print:

Electronic:

Audiovisuals:

Equipment:

Product or Culminating Activity: A description of the student activity, product, or work that makes clear student learning.

Assessment Overview: A description of the student activity, product, or work that is assessed during the unit, with notation of who assesses it and how is it assessed. Assessment tool(s) (rubric, checklist, or other) are included where available.

Adaptations and Extensions: Suggestions of other activities that might extend from this unit (such as speakers or additional products) and how the unit might be adapted to meet the needs of students who are exceptional learners, whether challenged or gifted, as well as those with varied learning styles.

Attachments: Handouts, graphic organizers, and rubrics.

INFORMATION POWER

The Nine Information Literacy Standards
for Student Learning

Excerpted with permission from Chapter 2, "Information Literacy Standards for Student Learning," of *Information Power: Building Partnerships for Learning* (AASL, 1998).

Information Literacy

Standard 1: The student who is information literate accesses information efficiently and effectively.

Standard 2: The student who is information literate evaluates information critically and competently.

Standard 3: The student who is information literate uses information accurately and creatively.

Independent Learning

Standard 4: The student who is an independent learner is information literate and pursues information related to personal interests.

Standard 5: The student who is an independent learner is information literate and appreciates literature and other creative expressions of information.

Standard 6: The student who is an independent learner is information literate and strives for excellence in information seeking and knowledge generation.

Social Responsibility

Standard 7: The student who contributes positively to the learning community and to society is information literate and recognizes the importance of information to a democratic society.

Standard 8: The student who contributes positively to the learning community and to society is information literate and practices ethical behavior in regard to information and information technology.

Standard 9: The student who contributes positively to the learning community and to society is information literate and participates effectively in groups to pursue and generate information.

American Association of School Librarians and Association for Educational Communication. *Information Power: Building Partnerships for Learning*. Chicago: American Library Association, 1998.

Figure 4.X **Blank Template**

Unit Title
Library Media Specialist Name and Title
Teacher Name(s) and Title
School Name
School Address
School Phone Number
Library Media Specialist E-mail Address

Grade Level:

Unit Overview:

Time Frame:

Content Area Standards:

Information Power Information Literacy Standards and Indicators:

Cooperative Teaching Plan:

    Library Media Specialist Will:

    Teacher(s) Will:

Resources:

Product or Culminating Activity:

Assessment Overview:

Adaptations and Extensions:

Attachments:

Artistic Connections

Ann Marie Pipkin, Library Media Specialist
Ben Rigsby, Susan Ripp, Hank Simpson: Art Teachers
James Knowles, Artist-in-Residence
Hoover High School
1000 Buccaneer Drive, Hoover, Alabama 35244
205-439-1242
apipkin@hoover.k12.al.us

Grade Level: 9–12

Unit Overview: In Artistic Connections, high school students focus on researching a specific art media and/or movement, integrating science, math, history, language, and the arts in their research. Students then produce designs recreating works of representative art and revealing the integration of the disciplines. Designs are submitted in a contest and judged by an independent committee. With the help of the artist-in-residence, students in AP Art transform the selected entries into a 10-panel mural displayed in the media center. Artistic Connections with broad community support includes several activities that are part of a grant written to secure funds for the various projects.

Time Frame: 6–9 months

Content Area Standards: Alabama Department of Education, Visual Arts Content Standards
<http://www.alsde.edu/html/sections/doc=download.asp?section=54&id=413>.
(Note: No indicators currently available)

Visual Arts Grades 9–12
Technique and Processes
Standard 3 (Proficient) Use appropriate media, techniques, or processes to solve visual arts problems to communicate ideas.
Standard 4 (Advanced) Produce artwork of exceptional quality to communicate ideas in at least one visual arts medium.

Design Elements and Principles
Standard 8 (Proficient) Use the principles of design and elements of art to solve specific visual arts problems in creating works of art.

History and Culture
Standard 12 (Proficient) Research the characteristics and purposes of a variety of interrelated historical and cultural works of art.
Standard 14 (Proficient) Analyze the historical and cultural influences and aesthetics of selected works of art.

Evaluation
Standard 20 (Advanced) Describe origins of specific images and ideas and explain why they are important in the work being examined and in the artwork of others.

Criticism

Standard 22 (Proficient) Describe specific works and show how they relate to historical and cultural context.

Connections

Standard 25 (Proficient) Compare characteristics of visual arts with the ideas, issues, or themes in the humanities or science within a given historical period.

Information Power Information Literacy Standards and Indicators: 1.1, 1.3, 1.4, 1.5, 2.1, 2.4, 3.1, 3.2, 3.3, 3.4, 9.1, 9.2, 9.3, 9.4

Cooperative Teaching Plan:

Library Media Specialist Will:

- Secure funds for art materials for the mural, artist-in-residence, and awards.
- Meet with teachers interested in participating in the program to select resources that will be used in the classroom as well as in the media center.
- Work with teachers to establish a timeline.
- Work with students in the media center to locate print and nonprint images for their designs.
- Select mural committee to judge submissions. (Committee includes the media specialist, the artist-in-residence, a representative from the art community, a parent, an administrator, and a faculty representative from each department.)
- Work with various community partners to supply awards for students whose images are chosen—plaques, pictures, banquet, etc.
- Contact media for coverage of various events.
- Work with artist-in-residence on mural: purchase of materials, production, and hanging.

Content/Subject Teacher Will:

- Meet with the library media specialist to view resources and schedule library visits.
- Choose several artistic, scientific, historical, etc. time periods on which students focus.
- Guide students in the media center to transform their research into visual aspects before making sketches for their submissions.
- Evaluate students' successful integration of historical and cultural aspects of eras.
- Provide material for the students to make the designs.
- Provide sketches of the designs for judging.
- Establish criteria for judging designs for final mural project.

Art History Resources:

Print

Print resources include a variety of art history reference books and books on different cultures, scientific discoveries and inventions, famous people, art in museums, and tessellations, such as:

Bazin, Germain. *A Concise History of World Sculpture*. New York: Fine Art Books, 1981.
Boardman, John, ed. *The Oxford History of Classical Art*. Oxford: Oxford University Press, 1993.
Dyson, James. *A History of Great Inventions*. New York: Carroll and Graf, 2001.
Frazier, Nancy. *The Penguin Concise Dictionary of Art History*. New York: Penguin, 2000.

Janson, H. W. *A History of Art.* New York: Harry N. Abrams, 2001.

Magill, Frank, ed. *Great Events from History: Arts and Culture Series.* Pasadena: Salem Press, 1993.

Turner, Jane Shoaf, ed. *Dictionary of Art.* New York: Groveart, 1996.

Electronic

Note: Electronic resources include encyclopedias and Web sites. Most Web sites can be found by searching for "art history" with any favorite search engine.

"Art." *World InfoZone.* 24 July 2002
               <http://www.worldinfozone.com/infozone.php?section=Art>.

"Art and Culture: Visual Arts: Websites." *EDSITEment.* 24 July 2002
               <http://edsitement.neh.fed.us/tab_websites.asp>.

"Art and Music Resources." *TEAMS Distance Learning.* 24 July 2002
               <http://teams.lacoe.edu/documentation/places/art.html>.

ArtLex. 5 June 2002. 24 July 2002 <http://www.artlex.com>.

WebMuseum, Paris. 17 July 2002. 22 July 2002 <http://www.ibiblio.org/wm>.

Audiovisual

Audiovisuals include those on the different art or historical movements: Ancient Greece, Ancient Rome, Baroque, Enlightenment, Renaissance, Middle Ages, Pre-Modern Era, Romanticism, Pop Art, Modern Art, etc., and include:

The History Of Art. Videocassette. Films for the Humanities & Sciences, 1999.

History Of Western Art. 6 videocassettes. Ambrose Video, 1999.

Landmarks Of Western Art. 6 videocassettes. Kultur, 1999.

Story of Painting. 5 videocassettes. BBC Video, 1997.

Supplies

Art Supplies include the necessary materials for making designs and the mural such as clay, canvas, brushes, paints, drawing paper, etc. Supplies for recognition and hanging should also be included.

Equipment

Computers with Internet access, a scanner, color printer and a copy machine make research and the saving of visual research easier but are not essential.

Grant Writing Resources:

Print

Bauer, David. *The "How To" Grants Manual: Successful Grantseeking Techniques For Obtaining Public And Private Grants.* Washington, D.C.: Oryx Press, 1999.

The Big Book of Library Grant Money 2002–2003. Chicago: American Library Association, 2001. (Note: the best print source for grant writing for libraries, authoritative, up-to-the minute, and library-specific.)

Electronic Resources

"ALA Awards, Grants, and Scholarships." *American Library Association*. December 2001. 24 July 2002 <http://www.ala.org/work/awards/>.

"Funding Opportunities." *U.S. Department of Education, Office of Educational Research and Improvement*. 24 April 2002. 24 July 2002 <http://www.ed.gov/offices/OERI/funding.html>.

"Grants and Contracts" *U.S. Department of Education*. 24 July 2002 <http://www.ed.gov/topics/topics.jsp?&top=Grants+%26+Contracts>.

SchoolGrants. 24 July 2002 <http://www.schoolgrants.org/>.

Product or Culminating Activity: Students make sketches of images from their research on artistic, scientific, historical, etc., time periods in order to submit as an entry for possible inclusion in a 5' by 30' mural produced by AP Art students. Sketches may also be used as the basis for a class project such as producing tiles, models, tessellations, book covers, etc.

Assessment Overview: Sketches are judged by an independent committee that looks for clarity and also a broad representation of all subjects in the curriculum. The sketches should cover a number periods of history, art, science, literature, and mathematics. If their sketches/designs are selected, students see their sketches transformed into the mural. The students working on the mural and the contest winners are honored at a banquet.

Extensions: Art Connections describes only the mural production aspect of a much broader unit.

At the beginning of this project, other teachers are encouraged to integrate art into their curriculum and to develop lesson plans using the media center for student research relating art to their subject matter. Math teachers may have their students work on tessellations. Science teachers may have their students work on inventions. Submitting a design need not be dependent on a student being a member of an art class.

Using the finished mural, students may develop a legend linking the product with the various images and giving recognition to the original art objects and paintings. This would address additional information literacy standards dealing with copyright and the ethical use of the images. In addition, using the finished mural, teachers may develop art lessons dealing with the elements of line, shape, texture, color, value, space and principles of unity, emphasis, balance, variety, movement, and proportion for critical viewing.

Because the mural cuts across all curriculum areas, lesson plans may also be developed to focus on the various aspects of history, science, and mathematics researched and may then be integrated with the literature of the different periods as well. Additional lessons may include upper-level art students assisting lower-level art students in designing a rendering of the mural in another medium, art students conducting tours of the mural for elementary groups, English classes writing critical analysis papers of the mural, and journalism classes critiquing the mural.

Figure 4.1   **Artistic Connections**

Three by Three Art Worksheet

Directions: Select three ages or movements in art and find three examples from each time period. All designs must include a written explanation of the images depicted and why the image is important. Attach explanations and pictures of your examples.

Ages and movements may include, but are not limited to, the following:

Prehistoric, Egyptian, Greek, Roman, Pre-Columbian, Middle Ages, Renaissance, Baroque, Neoclassicism, Romanticism, Realism, Art Nouveau, Photography, Impressionism, Post-Impressionism, Neo-Impressionism, Fauvism, Cubism, Futurism, Constructivism, Precisionism, Expressionism, De Stijl, DADA, Surrealism, Ashcan School, Abstract Expressionism, Color Field Painting, Hard Edge Painting, Pop Art, Minimalism, Conceptual Art, Photo Realism, Neo-expressionism, Post-Modern Art.

Name of Age or Movement	Dates of Age or Movement	Titles of Examples

Note: Art terms and examples might be changed to inventions or mathematical formulas. For example: name of invention, name of age/scientific movement, pictures of invention.

Figure 4.2   **Artistic Connections**

Timeline for Mural Project and Lesson Plans

August   Teachers from all subject areas are invited to join the mural committee in order to implement submission of ideas for art murals and to formulate competition guidelines. They receive professional development credit for work done after school on this project.

The committee includes the library media specialist, the artist-in-residence, a representative from the art community, a parent, an administrator, and a faculty representative from each department.

Launch contest. Contest guidelines are provided to all teachers, and participation is encouraged through announcements in the school and community newspapers, feature stories by the school broadcasting department, and flyers and posters distributed to all teachers in the school. (See attached flyer.)

September   Content/Subject teachers and library media specialist collaborate as students research art forms through the ages in subject classes and in the media center.

October 1   Deadline for students to submit proposed designs.

October   Mural committee meets to select designs that will be included in the mural. Collectively, the committee also submits a design proposal for the entire mural.

November–February

The mural is created by students under the supervision of the artist-in-residence who will receive a stipend and/or professional development credit. The artist-in-residence is responsible for the purchase of materials, production, and the hanging of the finished mural in the high school media center.

February   Dedication of mural

March   Curriculum design workshop for art teachers to write lesson plans on elements of art incorporating the mural.

April   Complete all paperwork needed to satisfy requirements to finish grant.

Note: This timeline does not include the deadlines that are demanded by individual grants, such as the date for submission of the proposal (beginning of process) and the date for evaluation (end of the process) of the finished project. Nor does the timeline include any pre-proposal work, such as obtaining in-kind permission or securing matching funds. Aside from the actual activities, these details can extend the project for two years from beginning to end.

| Figure 4.3 | **Artistic Connections** |

Flyer

MuralMakers Contest

Submit your design, which will be used for a large mural in the Media Center.

This design should depict art in history, math, social studies, science, foreign language, business, physical education, English, music or drama.

All designs must include a written explanation of the image depicted and why the image is important.

Become a part of History at Hoover High School

- Open to all students
- Designs should be on letter or legal size paper in black and white or color
- Name, address, and telephone number on the back
- Turn in designs to the Media Center
- **Deadline:** October 1

> **Students whose designs are selected are invited to a**
> # CELEBRATION
> **immediately following the contest and to a**
> # FORMAL DEDICATION
> **in the spring**

Examples:

- Artistic renditions of an important personality, place, event, discovery, etc.
  Examples: Einstein, Waterloo, cotton gin, discovery of America, pyramids
- Symbols or images, words or phrases depicting a specific discipline and/or specific time
  Examples: chemical formulas, graphs, microscopic images

> **All submissions are considered ideas,**
> **which may be adapted to fit the overall design of the mural.**

Figure 4.4 **Artistic Connections**

Rubric for Class Project: Mural Contest

Category	Excellent	Good	Satisfactory	Needs Improvement
Submission Requirements	Has met all requirements	Missing one component	Missing two components	Missing three components
Planning/ Research	Detailed written plan	Written outline	Some evidence of planning	No evidence of planning
Curricular Relevance	Representative of 3 subject areas	Representative of 2 subject areas	Representative of 1 subject area	No tie in to curriculum evident
Craftsmanship/ Skill	Beautifully, patiently done	Lacks the finishing touches	Adequate, a bit careless	Lack of pride in finished work
Knowledge Gained	Can accurately answer 100% of the questions about the design content	Can accurately answer 80% of the questions about the design content	Can accurately answer 60% of the questions about the design content	Lacks knowledge about the design content

Note: This is a generic rubric. For examples of rubrics or to develop one that fits your project better, you may use Rubistar at the 4teachers Web site <http://www.4teachers.org/technology/erica4/index.shtml>

Asteroid Impact!

Lynn Rutan and Sharon Iverson, Librarians
Chad Miller, Ninth Grade Science Teacher
Macatawa Bay School
3700 140th Avenue, Holland, Michigan 49424
616-786-2186
frutan@novagate.com

Grade Level: 9

Unit Overview: Students in a ninth grade heterogeneously grouped general education introductory Science class receive an e-mail from NASA appealing to all educational institutions for help in creating solutions to a newly discovered crisis facing the Earth. An asteroid has been discovered that will collide with the Earth in the near future. Students, working in groups of four to five, propose a course of action to prevent human extinction. They direct their own learning by designing their approach and solution. Computers are the means to gather (Internet and e-mail), communicate (e-mail) and organize (Inspiration, word processing, *PowerPoint*, etc.) information for the purpose of making a presentation.

Time Frame: 7–9 weeks

Content Area Standards: Michigan Curriculum Framework
<http://www.michigan.gov/documents/MichiganCurriculumFramework_8172_7.pdf>

Science Content Strands

Strand I: Constructing New Scientific Knowledge
Standard I.1: Constructing New Scientific Knowledge. All students will ask questions that help them learn about the world; design and conduct investigations using appropriate methodology and technology; learn from books and other sources of information; communicate their findings using appropriate technology; and reconstruct previously learned knowledge.
I.1.1. Develop questions or problems for investigation that can be answered empirically.
I.1.2. Suggest empirical tests of hypothesis.
I.1.3. Design and conduct scientific investigations.
I.1.7. Gather and synthesize information from books and other sources of information.
I.1.8. Discuss topics in groups by being able to restate or summarize what others have said, ask for clarification or elaboration, and take alternative perspectives.
I.1.9. Reconstruct previously learned knowledge.

Strand IV: Using Scientific Knowledge in Physical Science
Standard IV.1: Matter and Energy. All students will measure and describe the things around us; explain what the world around us is made of; identify and describe forms of energy; and explain how electricity and magnetism interact with matter.

IV.1.1. Describe and compare objects in terms of mass, volume, and density.

Standard IV.2: Changes in Matter. All students will investigate, describe and analyze ways in which matter changes; describe how living things and human technology change matter and transform energy; explain how visible changes in matter are related to atoms and molecules; and how changes in matter are related to changes in energy.
IV.2.1. Explain how mass is conserved in physical and chemical changes.
IV.2.7. Describe energy changes associated with physical and chemical changes.

Standard IV.3: Motion of Objects. All students will describe how things around us move and explain why things move as they do; demonstrate and explain how we control the motions of objects; and relate motion to energy and energy conversions.
IV.3.1. Perform measurements and calculations to describe the speed and direction of an object.
IV.3.2. Describe that whenever one object exerts a force on a second object, the second object exerts an equal and opposite force on the first object.
IV.3.4. Explain energy conversions in moving objects and in simple machines.

Strand V: Using Scientific Knowledge in Earth Science
Standard V.1: The Geosphere. All students will describe the earth's surface; describe and explain how the earth's features change over time; and analyze effects of technology on the earth's surface and resources.
V.1.2. Use the plate tectonics theory to explain features of the earth's surface and geological phenomena and describe evidence for the plate tectonics theory.

Standard V.4: The Solar System, Galaxy and Universe. All students will compare and contrast our planet and sun to other planets and star systems; describe and explain how objects in the solar system move; explain scientific theories as to the origin of the solar system; and explain how we learn about the universe.
V.4.3. Describe the position and motion of our solar system in the universe.
V.4.4. Explain current scientific thinking about how the solar system formed.
V.4.6. Explain how technology and scientific inquiry have helped us learn about the universe.

Information Power Information Literacy Standards and Indicators: 1.1, 1.2, 1.3, 1.4, 1.5, 2.1, 2.2, 2.3, 2.4, 3.1, 3.2, 3.3, 3.4, 9.1, 9.2, 9.3, 9.4

Cooperative Teaching Plan:

Librarians Will:
■ Instruct students in Boolean searching techniques.
■ Instruct students in Internet site evaluation.
■ Facilitate student research strategy decisions. Guiding questions include:
  • What information do they already know?
  • What information is required?
  • What are the possible sources of information?
■ Assist students to locate and evaluate information sources as needed.
■ Assist students with bibliographic citations.

Teacher Will:

- Serve as a resource to students and monitor student progress.
- Instruct students in units on specific scientific topics.
- Randomly group students into teams of 5-6.
- Facilitate a brainstorming session using KWL to assess prior knowledge and information needed to begin work on the problem and complete the project.
- Allow students time to sketch out a possible solution and turn in a one-page proposal.
- Read regular reports sent by students via e-mail.
- In conjunction with students, develop a rubric for evaluation.
- In conjunction with students, determine due dates for e-mail reports and the rubric.
- Guide students in evaluating information located on the Internet for accuracy, authenticity and usefulness.
- Assist students in consulting with local as well as national experts.
- Introduce new challenges to re-focus and re-energize students.
- On student request, make resources available through the Internet student pages and mini-lessons.
- Monitor student progress.
- Instruct students in units on specific scientific topics.

Resources: This project is an online unit and was designed to allow flexibility for other teachers who may choose to use the unit. Access to Internet, e-mail, and computers with word processing, spread-sheet, presentation and Web page creation software are essential. Print resources will also be valuable. We suggest some of the following basic resources.

Print

Dasch, E. Julius, ed. *Earth Sciences for Students*. New York: Macmillan Reference, 1999.

Earth Sciences. Danbury, Connecticut: Grolier Educational, 2000.

Encyclopedia Americana. Danbury, Connecticut: Grolier, 2001.

Encyclopedia of Earth and Physical Sciences. New York: Marshall Cavendish, 1998.

Engelbert, Phillis, ed. *Astronomy & Space: From the Big Bang to the Big Crunch*. Detroit: Gale Research, 1997.

Engelbert, Phillis and Diane L. Dupuis. *Handy Space Answer Book*. Detroit: Visible Ink Press, 1998.

Engelbert, Phillis, ed. *UXL Science Fact Finder*. Detroit: Gale Research, 1998.

Gundersen, P. Erik. *Handy Physics Answer Book*. Detroit: Visible Ink Press, 1999.

Hitt, Robert, Jr., ed. *Outer Space*. Danbury, Connecticut: Grolier Educational, 1998.

New Book of Popular Science. Danbury, Connecticut: Grolier Educational, 2000.

Newton, David E., ed. *UXL Encyclopedia of Science*. Detroit: Gale Research, 1998.

Physics Matters. Danbury, Connecticut: Grolier Educational, 2001.

World Book Encyclopedia. Chicago: World Book, Inc., 2001.

Electronic

The following Internet resources are included on the project Web site:

Arnett, Bill. "The Nine Planets: A Multimedia Tour of the Solar System." *Bill Arnett*. 27 February 2001. 24 July 2002 <http://seds.lpl.arizona.edu/nineplanets/nineplanets/nineplanets.html#toc>.

"Classical Gas—Feline Reactions to Bearded Men." *Hot A.I.R.* 24 July 2002
   http://www.improbable.com/airchives/classical/cat/cat.html>.
"Collision Course: Bracing for an Asteroid Impact." *CNN*. 24 July 2002
   <http://www.cnn.com/TECH/space/9803/12/collision>.
Fox, Paul G. "Six Deadliest Sins of Presentations." *Fox Performance Training and Human
   Resource Services*. 24 July 2002
   <http://www.foxperformance.com/presentation4.html>.
"Introduction to Physical Science: Sir Isaac Newton." *Honolulu Community College*.
   24 July 2002
   <http://www.hcc.hawaii.edu/hccinfo/instruct/div5/sci/sci122/newton/newtlaw.html>.
"NASA Ames Research Center Annual Space Settlement Contest." *Ralston Middle School
   Industrial Technology*. 24 July 2002
   <http://www.belmont.k12.ca.us/ralston/programs/itech/SpaceSettlement/Contest/
   contests.html>.
"Planetary Sciences." *National Space Science Data Center*. 3 July 2001. 24 July 2002
   <http://nssdc.gsfc.nasa.gov/planetary>.
Presentations.com. 24 July 2002 <http://www.presentations.com/presentations/index.jsp>.
Sagan, Carl. "Why Near Earth Objects?" *The Neo Pages:Planetary Society*. 24 July 2002
   <http://neo.planetary.org/ABCsOfNEOs/SaganWhy.html>.
"The Spacewatch Project." *Planetary Image Research Laboratory, The University of Arizona*.
   12 July 2002. 24 July 2002 <http://pirlwww.lpl.arizona.edu/Spacewatch/>.
Templeton, Brad. "A Brief Introduction to Copyright." *Brad Templeton's Home Page*.
   24 July 2002 <http://www.templetons.com/brad/copyright.html>.
Templeton, Brad. "Ten Big Myths about Copyright Explained." *Brad Templeton's Home Page*.
   9 January 2002 <http://www.templetons.com/brad/copymyths.html>.
Tobin, Isaac. *Newton's Three Laws of Motion*. 24 July 2002
   <http://www.aloha.com/~isaac/3laws/3lmid.htm>.
Umbach, Ken. "California's Velcro Crop Under Challenge (1993)." *Ken Umbach's Award
   Winning Home Page*. 24 July 2002 < http://home.inreach.com/kumbach/velcro.html>.
"The United States Copyright Office." *Library of Congress*. 24 July 2002
   <http://www.loc.gov/copyright/>.
"Welcome to the Planets." *NASA Planetary Data System*. 24 July 2002
   <http://pds.jpl.nasa.gov/planets/welcome.htm>.

Product or Culminating Activity: Students develop a presentation that reflects their group solution to the problem. Students may choose the form of their presentation. They are guided toward *PowerPoint*, videotaped speech, word-processed document, flyer via *Microsoft Publisher*, or Web pages using *FrontPage*. Presentations are made to a high school Advanced Placement class who serve as a screening board affiliated with NASA. The class will select the best three solutions. The teacher will also evaluate all groups' solutions based on the rubric. The best three solutions will be presented to the local screening board who will select the best solutions to be forwarded to NASA. Following the conclusion of this unit, students will continue to monitor the path of near earth asteroids. Students recognize that their efforts to devise effective and realistic solutions to the problem of an asteroid on a collision course with Earth could preserve not only their future but that of all people on Earth.

Assessment Overview: Students will be assessed on their initial proposal, regular e-mail reports, and the quality of their final presentation according to the rubric designed by students and teacher.

Note: This project was developed as a part of a LInC class using engaged learning methods. The LInC classes are a joint project of the Fermi National Accelerator Laboratory Education Office, the United States Department of Energy, the Illinois State Board of Education, North Central Regional Educational Laboratory (NCREL) and the National Science Foundation.

The unit was designed as an online project and can be accessed at:

<http://www-ed.fnal.gov/lincon/w99/projects/michigan/asteroidimpact/home.html>

| Figure 4.5 | Asteroid Impact! |

Student Introduction

Asteroid Impact!
"The clock is ticking. Will you save the Earth?"

The Armageddon Project

Help! Top Secret documents from the Pentagon reveal that there is a very real possibility of an asteroid colliding with Earth! Several well-known scientists are claiming that there may be as many as thousands of asteroids, yet unknown to us, destined to destroy this planet. You, as members of the Earth Life Survival Committee (a division of the National Security Council) are responsible for researching and reporting to the nation on the dangers that this presents and what course we as a planet might take for survival.

One such asteroid's name is Eros. Scientists once thought that this asteroid might hit Earth and have been studying it for years. We even sent a satellite to investigate its characteristics. In the long run, Eros did not hit Earth. The newest information, however, shows that there are many others like Eros that we have not yet even discovered. In your research you are to discover what these asteroids are like and what methods we might be able to use to stop them from wiping out life on Earth.

When you have gathered enough basic information, you will be given class time to work in groups to devise your solution. Each group will be responsible for presenting its solution to the N.A.S.A. Screening Committee and convincing them to use it.

It would be to your advantage to take some time to assign roles to team members so that everyone is doing his or her share. When all of the solutions are prepared, the committee will decide on the best solution.

Your final solution must contain references to each of the major "themes" of the objectives from your "Asteroids Unit Objectives" sheet. These are:

Themes	Objectives
Density	#2
Energy (Transfer and Transformations)	#5-8, #15
Physical Change and States of Matter	#9-14
Earth's Structure	#16-17
Biomes and Adaptations	#18-20
Origin of our Solar System and our Universe	#26-27
Celestial Objectives (Nebulae, Stars, Novas, etc.)	#28-29

PREPARE NOW...FOR THE END MAY BE NEAR!

| Figure 4.6 | Asteroid Impact! |

Unit Objectives

To prove that you have learned the material in this unit you will:

1. Distinguish between mass and weight and calculate an object's weight.
2. Calculate the density of liquids and solids ($D = m/V$).
3. Know and apply Newton's Three Laws of Motion (Inertia, $F = ma$, Action-Reaction).
4. Perform measurements and calculations to describe the motion of an object ($v = d/t$, $a = v/t$).
5. Explain what is meant by energy and give several common forms.
6. State and explain the Law of Conservation of Energy and how energy is transferred and transformed.
7. Describe and explain energy transformations (potential to kinetic to thermal).
8. Explain the mechanisms of heat transfer (conduction, convection, radiation).
9. Explain what is meant by a physical change and give common examples.
10. Know the states of matter and describe the characteristics of each.
11. Explain the relationship between physical changes and atom and molecule arrangement.
12. Describe the energy changes in matter as it undergoes phase changes.
13. Explain several physical changes associated with thermal energy (condensation, fusion, vaporization).
14. Identify the states of matter in each region of a cooling curve.
15. Discuss energy transfer and transformation from an asteroid to other systems in a collision.
16. Explain the composition of the Earth (crust, mantle, core).
17. Describe evidence that supports the theory of Plate Tectonics.
18. List 8 major biomes and the characteristics of each.
19. Locate the major biomes of North America on a map.
20. Understand and explain how organisms adapt to changes in their environment.
21. Compare the characteristics of the Sun, Moon, and Earth.
22. Explain the causes of the seasons on Earth.
23. Explain the causes of the phases of the Moon.
24. Compare and contrast the characteristics (orbit, mass, moons) and surface conditions (temperature, atmosphere) of the planets in our solar system.
25. Describe the make-up and orbits of asteroids and comets.
26. Describe the theory of the origin of our solar system and objects (sun, planets, moons, asteroids, comets, etc.) in it.
27. Describe the theory of the origin of the Universe.
28. Visualize and categorize celestial objects (nebula, stars, novas, black holes, etc.).
29. Diagram the life cycle of stars.
30. Describe the use of technology and scientific inquiry in learning about our universe.

Figure 4.7 **Asteroid Imapct!**

Energy Research Assignment

1. Define energy.

2. Brainstorm at least 5 common forms of energy.

3. In all capital letters, write the Law of Conservation of Energy in the space provided.

4. Explain what happens to energy when it appears to have been destroyed.

5. How are kinetic and potential energy different from one another?

6. What is the potential energy of a 2 kg book on shelf 1.25 m above the floor? No sentence needed, just show your work.

7. What is the kinetic energy of a 900 kg car traveling down a highway at 72 Km/h?

8. What is the definition of "temperature?"

9. Explain thermal energy as if you were talking to a sixth grader.

10. Define "heat."

11. What is thermodynamics? Relate this to the Law of Conservation of Energy.

12.Name and explain the three mechanisms of heat transfer.

Figure 4.8   **Asteroid Impact!**

Assignments: "What Do We Have to Do?"

Check here for the assignments due each week. Remember, you will have only two class periods in the computer lab to complete this work. Some of the assignments listed must be completed in the classroom and some must be done at home.

Week Ending on:	Assignment
	❑ Type and print a *Word* document stating the names of everyone on your team. Turn this in to your teacher. (**One per group**) ❑ Consider roles and jobs that people will have to perform for your group to come up with and present a successful solution. ❑ Research the meaning of "density" on the Internet. Prepare a two-word definition (in your own words) for density. ❑ Complete the Density Lab and turn in the Density Homework assignment. ❑ Complete the Newton's 2nd Law Lab and turn in the write-up.
	❑ Complete the Energy Assignment #1. ❑ Complete the Toy Lab for Energy Transfers and Transformations. Write-up due by end of week. ❑ Brainstorm some roles that will have to be filled by your group in order to successfully save the world. Decide among the group who will take on which roles. Finally, e-mail your teacher a list of who will be responsible for which roles. **NOTE: EVERYONE IS RESPONSIBLE FOR THE RESEARCH! DON'T ASSIGN IT AS A ROLE BECAUSE IT IS EVERYONE'S JOB!**
	❑ In a one-page paper (typed, double spaced, 12 pt. font.) describe as many energy transfers and transformations as you can think of that would occur as the asteroid hit the earth. ❑ Complete the States of Matter Lab and write-up. ❑ Brainstorm criteria that you think are fair ways for your teacher to evaluate your solutions and presentations. To do this, check out the rubric entitled "How Will We Be Graded?" This is a template for you to suggest your own criteria for grading. You may have no more than 8 criteria and you must address my "Big Three!"

| Figure 4.9 | **Asteroid Impact!** |

Evaluating Internet Resources: "Have I Found a Good Web Page?"

Anyone can publish on the Internet. You can too. It's very important to examine carefully the information you find on any Internet Web page. Take a look at the following Web pages. Evaluate the following two Web pages using the questions listed in the table below.

- *California's Velcro Crop Under Challenge* <http://home.inreach.com/kumbach/velcro.html>
- *Why Near-Earth Objects?* <http://neo.planetary.org/ABCsOfNEOs/SaganWhy.html>

Authority	Is the author or organizational author identified?	❏ Yes ❏ No
	Does the author list occupation, education, or other credentials?	❏ Yes ❏ No
	Is the author the original creator of the piece?	❏ Yes ❏ No
Accuracy	Are the sources of the facts documented?	❏ Yes ❏ No
	Can you verify the facts from other sources?	❏ Yes ❏ No
Audience	Who is the Web page designed for?	_____
Bias	Is the purpose of the page to inform?	❏ Yes ❏ No
	Is the purpose of the page to advocate a position?	❏ Yes ❏ No
	Is the purpose of the page to sell?	❏ Yes ❏ No
	Does the purpose affect the accuracy of the information?	❏ Yes ❏ No
	Does the author distinguish fact from opinion?	❏ Yes ❏ No
Currency	When was the Web page created?	_____
	When was the page last updated?	_____
Design	Does the page take a long time to load?	❏ Yes ❏ No
	Is the page easy to navigate?	❏ Yes ❏ No
	Do the graphics enhance or distract?	❏ Yes ❏ No
	Are the links helpful and relevant?	❏ Yes ❏ No

Figure 4.10   Asteroid Impact!

Rubric Page: "How Will We Be Graded?"

The following is an outline of what you are expected to learn in this project. We will work as a class to determine what is quality work in each of these categories.

Each student will...	0	1	2	3
Use the scientific method to develop a solution to a problem.				
Design and conduct investigations to solve a problem.				
Measure and calculate properties of matter such as velocity, acceleration, mass and force.				
Predict and calculate potential and kinetic energy.				
Describe conversions of energy (i.e. mechanical to thermal).				
Demonstrate knowledge of the relationship between temperature and states of matter.				
Calculate and apply Newton's 3 Laws of Motion.				
Describe the Earth's three layers with a special focus on the crust.				
Describe our solar system in terms of its origin and components.				
Describe the planets in terms of orbits and physical characteristics.				
Use *PowerPoint*, e-mail, and search engines and demonstrate skill in Web site content evaluation.				

Your project grade will be based on the result of this rubric. You will also be evaluated based on your weekly correspondence with your teacher/library media specialist.

A Biome Vacation: Travel Brochures

Rebecca Blick, Library Media Specialist

Stacy Robins, Science Instructor

Washburn Rural High School

5900 SW 61st Street, Topeka, Kansas 66619

785-339-4100

blickbec@aw437.k12.ks.us

Grade Level: 9

Unit Overview: A Biome Vacation: Travel Brochures develops students' research skills and understanding of specific biome characteristics as they create trip enticer travel brochures. Embedded within a high school biology course, this project is the culminating activity for an ecology unit. Students learn research skills through library and Internet use and become proficient in the use of *Microsoft Publisher* software when creating their brochures. The project provides opportunities for creativity as students reveal their understanding of science principles.

Time Frame: 3 weeks. Ecology unit requires two weeks in the classroom for introduction of concepts and principles and one week for research and production of the biome brochures.

Content Area Standards: Science Curriculum Guide, Business and Office Education Curriculum, Auburn-Washburn Public Schools, Topeka, Kansas (URL not available)

Science Program Outcomes:
1. A knowledge of the scientific process
2. An appreciation and curiosity of the natural world
3. A knowledge base and understanding of biological, physical and environmental/earth sciences

Biology I
1. Apply ecological interrelationships to global biomes and regional and local ecosystems.
   a. Recognize the seven biomes of the world and discriminate the individual characteristics of each.
   b. Identify the interaction of organisms within an ecosystem.
   c. Evaluate the interrelationships between abiotic factors and living organisms.
2. Demonstrate responsible behavior in relation to commitment and time management.
   a. Demonstrate consistent completion of assigned tasks.
   b. Perform work in a timely fashion.
   c. Demonstrate good attendance habits.

Business and Office Education Program Outcomes
1. The business-related and general education knowledge, skill, attitudes, and values necessary to be productive consumers and citizens.

2. The knowledge and skills necessary to obtain employment in a business-related field.
3. An appreciation for the necessity of lifelong learning.

Computer Technology
1. Demonstrate the use of software applications including word processing, spreadsheets, database management, electronic mail, Internet and operating systems.
2. Develop projects and products using a variety of software applications.
   a. open several programs at once
   b. copy from one program to another program
   c. use multi-tasking with numerous programs

Information Power Information Literacy Standards and Indicators: 1.1, 1.4, 1.5, 2.1, 2.4, 3.1, 3.2, 3.3, 3.4, 8.1, 8.2, 8.3

Cooperative Teaching Plan:

Library Media Specialist Will:
- Assemble library books and materials.
- Pre-search Internet sites.
- Introduce/demonstrate use of specific research sources.
- Assist students in using library and Internet resources.
- Introduce/instruct students in the use of Microsoft Publisher software to create brochures.
- Teach students to import graphics from Web sites.
- Provide format for crediting sources used in project.
- Collect and have available brochures, pamphlets, travel magazines and other paraphernalia from local travel agencies.

Teacher Will:
- Teach content for ecology unit prior to research phase.
- Communicate expectations for the assignment.
- Guide students in determining the appropriate biome type for their location.
- Assist students with information gathering from print and electronic resources.
- Assist students during production of brochures.
- Evaluate finished product.

Resources:
Print
Biomes of the World. Danbury, CT: Grolier Educational, 1999.

Sayre, April Pulley. *Exploring Earth's Biomes* (series). New York: Twenty-First-Century Books, 1994.

Weigel, Marlene. *UXL Encyclopedia of Biomes* (series). Detroit: Gale, 2000.

Electronic
"Biomes of the World." *MBGnet*. 24 July 2002 <http://mbgnet.mobot.org/sets/index.htm>.

Ciucci, Mary, Colleen McCartney, and Amy Warren. "Biome Basics." University of Richmond. 24 July 2002
   <http://oncampus.richmond.edu/academics/as/education/projects/webunits/biomes.html>.

Audiovisual

The Desert. Videocassette. Britannica, 1987.

Life on the Tundra. Videocassette. Britannica, 1987.

The Living Planet (series). Videocassette. Time Life Video, 1991. (Titles include: *The Margins of the Land*, *New Worlds*, *Seas of Grass*, *The Northern Forests*, *Sweet Fresh Water*, *The Frozen World*, *The Baking Deserts*)

Temperate Deciduous Forest. Videocassette. Britannica, 1987.

Tropical Rain Forest. Videocassette. Britannica, 1987.

Product or Culminating Activity: Each student chooses a specific world location and identifies the biome most prevalent in that place. He/she then researches both scientific and travel/tourist information for that place and creates a travel brochure to "advertise" it.

Assessment Overview: The pamphlet is assessed by the classroom teacher using a rubric.

Adaptations and Extensions: This unit format has been successfully adapted for use with world geography. Students research a country and create a brochure, but the emphasis is on geography and culture rather than environment.

Figure 4.11 **A Biome Vacation: Travel Brochures**

Requirements

Choose a place in the world that you would like to visit or somewhere you have been. After you decide on a destination, your task will be to find out what type of biome exists in this spot.

BROCHURE: Once these two tasks are accomplished, create a travel brochure that entices people to visit while presenting information about the characteristics of that biome. You will make the brochure appealing to travelers by using color and other elements of visual appeal to cause travelers to want to read it as soon as they see it while you also teach them about the biome. Include all of these items in the brochure:

- The name and location of the biome;
- The amount and types of precipitation the biome receives and when it occurs;
- The average temperature (if possible day/night and seasonal);
- The length of growing seasons (or different seasons-North America has four);
- Any unique characteristics of the biome;
- Plants found in the biome (minimum of seven);
- Animals found in the biome (minimum of seven).

VACATION PLAN: You will also develop a vacation plan for a city within your biome. Include the following:

- Fun activities;
- Eating spots or restaurants;
- Places to stay overnight.

In order to do this, you will locate a real city within the biome where a traveler can stay. Have fun with this part. Use your imagination and come up with a great vacation plan. Remember, to attract visitors, it must be appealing. See teacher for some travel magazines to show you how to develop a vacation package and some example brochures from years past.

The more creativity and time you put into this project, the better the results will be. You will create your brochure using *Microsoft Publisher* (or you may use templates available in most word processing software). Be sure to include pictures. You will receive instructions on using *Publisher* and two class periods of work time for the creation of the brochure itself.

BROCHURE LAYOUT: See the plan for layout of your brochure. You may also include a one-panel insert with "tourist information" if your brochure is heavy on pictures or you run out of room using the model. The tourist information should include things to do in the biome, places to stay and eat, attractions, and approximate cost for the vacation. You may include as many pictures as you wish. The layout is just a guide! Some students choose to write descriptions of plants, animals, weather, etc., and some choose to write brief descriptions with actual photos.

Figure 4.11   **(continued from page 57)**

Page 1 (outside of brochure/cover)

Left panel (column 1) Include the following:	Center panel (column 2) Include the following:	Right panel/Cover (column 3) Include the following:
Climate Precipitation Temperature Growing season Unique Characteristics Interesting facts and pictures not included in requirements may be placed in this space	Resources List in alphabetical order using MLA format.	Name of Biome Type Beautiful or exciting picture! City and Country Student Name Course Date

Page 2 (inside of brochure)

Left panel (column 1) Include the following:	Center panel (column 2) Include the following:	Right panel (column 3) Include the following:
Plants List or describe at least 7 plants. Include a representative illustration, or pictures of each species listed.	Tourist Information Here…Or… Information about the biome: What conditions created this biome? What other spots in the world have similar biomes? Why?	Animals List or describe at least 7 animals. Include a representative illustration or pictures of each species listed.

Figure 4.12   *A Biome Vacation: Travel Brochures*

Travel Brochure Grading Rubric

Name _____   Hour _____

Not Present:	**0**
Poor:	**1**
Good	**2**
Excellent	**3**

Content:

Amount of precipitation _____

Average temperature _____

Length of seasons/what kinds _____

Unique characteristics of the biome _____

Plants (7 minimum) _____

Animals (7 minimum) _____

Appearance:

Typed/Neat _____

Pictures (specific, not only clipart) _____

Resources with correct MLA format _____

Creativity/Interest _____

Instructions followed (format plan) _____

Vacation Plan:

Approximate costs for vacation included _____

Hotels/places to stay _____

Places to eat _____

Attractions/things to do _____

Total Points: _____

Capstone Project

Mary Alice Anderson, Lead Media Specialist
Social Studies, Industrial Technology, Communications, Science,
Language Arts Teachers
Winona Middle School
1570 Homer Road, Winona MN 55987
507-494-1050
maryalic@wms.luminet.net

Grade Levels: 6–8

Unit Overview: The Capstone Project is a technology-based multi-grade, multidisciplinary unit that ensures equity in instruction and opportunity while facilitating a high degree of curriculum integration. It allows students to meet a state Technology Applications graduation standard that requires students to "use appropriate technology to access, evaluate, and organize information and to produce products." They produce and save: a word processing document, a digitized self image, a multimedia project, a spreadsheet chart/graph, and a database, using appropriate keyboarding techniques. The final product is the Capstone Portfolio, a culmination of previous work. Individual components are revised as student skill progresses, technology changes, and the teaching team structure changes.

Time Frame: Individual tasks: 1–3 weeks. Full Capstone project: three years (three tasks in sixth grade, one task in seventh grade, and two tasks in eighth grade). Students store their completed work in their personal folders on the school's server.

Content Standards: The Minnesota Graduation Standards <http://cfl.state.mn.us/GRAD/cur_rule.html>

Learning Area Nine: Resource Management, Middle-level content standards

D. Technology applications. A student shall use appropriate technology to access, evaluate, and organize information and to produce products by:
   1. gathering and evaluating information from electronic sources;
   2. applying appropriate technology processes to an identified need or problem;
   3. producing products and selecting language, format, and graphics appropriate for purpose and audience by using word processing, graphics, multimedia, spreadsheets, and databases; and
   4. maintaining, using, or creating a technological system.

Learning Area Two: Write and Speak, Middle-level content standards

A. Writing. A student shall demonstrate for a variety of academic and technical purposes, situations, and audiences the ability to write:
   3. an idea or opinion that:
      a. gives a rationale that includes reasons to support or oppose the opinion;
      b. uses evidence to support the idea; and
      c. has correct spelling and mechanics.

Learning Area Five: Inquiry, Middle-level content standards.

A. Direct observation. A student shall demonstrate the ability to gather information to answer a scientific or social science question through:

    1. direct observations, including framing a question, collecting and recording data, displaying data in appropriate format, looking for patterns in observable data, relating findings to new situations or large group findings, answering a question or presenting a position using data, and identifying areas for further investigation.

Information Power Information Literacy Standards and Indicators: 1.1, 1.2, 1.3, 1.4, 1.5, 2.1, 2.2, 2.4, 3.1, 3.2, 3.3, 3.4, 4.2, 5.2, 5.3, 6.1, 6.2, 7.1, 7.2, 8.2, 8.3, 9.1, 9.2, 9.3

Cooperative Teaching Plan:

Media Specialist Will:

- Work with individual teachers or teams of teachers to develop the curriculum and teaching activities and to revise teaching activities as needed.
- Work with teachers to develop and modify assessments.
- Plan and implement staff development activities that help teachers become familiar with the technology and information resources.
- Stay abreast of changes in technologies and information technology that affect the project.
- Inform teachers of new resources in all formats.
- Maintain the school's Web site and links to resources.
- Purchase needed resources in all formats.
- Function as the project manager and coordinator to ensure that all tasks are scheduled, integrated into existing curriculum, and completed.
- Work with the district network specialist, technicians, and media center staff to ensure that all software and hardware is installed and operating.
- Develop teaching materials, handouts, and forms.
- Develop and maintain the project management system using *FileMaker Pro*.
- Co-teach individual portions of specific tasks as needed.
- Develop sample portfolios and assist with the final assessment.
- Work with the district curriculum director and report to the district curriculum committee to ensure project completion.

All Teachers Will:

- Acquire and maintain skills needed to implement the task.
- Work with media specialist to schedule and implement their portions of the project.
- Work with media specialist to make necessary revisions in teaching/learning activities.
- Teach, implement and assess their individual portions of the project.
- Record student scores in the project database.

Sixth Grade Social Studies Teachers Will:

- Meet with the media specialist to become familiar with new resources and schedule instructional, research, and lab time.
- Co-teach research skills, *HyperStudio*, scanning, and saving to the server.
- Oversee research activities with assistance from the media center.

Sixth Grade Language Arts Teachers Will:
- Introduce students to saving files to the shared server.
- Teach and assess the writing activity.
- Work with students in the labs as they complete word processing.
- Reinforce computer ethics and procedures for saving to the server.

Sixth Grade Communications Teachers Will:
- Enter student names in the *Type to Learn* Management system.
- Ensure that students complete required keyboarding lessons.
- Ask students to complete final keyboarding reflection and save it to their server space.

Sixth Grade Science Teachers Will:
- Plan and implement the meter/monitor electrical use study.
- With the media specialist, co-teach creation of spreadsheets and graphs.
- Ask students to save their final graphs in their server space.

Seventh Grade Social Studies Teachers Will:
- Direct students to use their geography textbook to gather and record data about countries.
- Work with the media specialist to co-teach database creation and data manipulation.
- Ask students to save their final database in their server space.

Eighth Grade Communications Technology Teachers Will:
- Facilitate student use of the digital camera.
- Review the use of *Adobe Photo Deluxe* for digital photo manipulation.
- Facilitate student creation of the Capstone *HyperStudio* portfolio.
- Encourage students to go beyond the minimal portfolio requirements.
- Assess the final portfolio and report the final assessment score.

Resources:

Print
A wide collection of individual print titles depending on student research choices in Task 1, including these titles and others:

Allen, Christine, and Anderson, Mary Alice, ed. "Famous People from Your State or City." *Skills for Life, Information Literacy for Grades 7–12*. Columbus, Ohio: Linworth Publishing, 1999, 102–107.

Anderson, Mary Alice, "The Media Center: School-Wide, Multi-Disciplinary Portfolios." *Multimedia Schools* 7.3 (May/June 2000): 20–24.

Anderson, Mary Alice, "The Media Center: The Evolution of a Curriculum: Yes, You Can Manage iMovie Projects with 170 Kids!" *Multimedia Schools* 9.4 (September 2002): 17–19.

Current Biography Yearbook. New York, New York: H.W. Wilson Company, 1940–present.

Junior Authors and Illustrators series. New York, New York: H.W. Wilson Company, 1951–2000.

Minnesota Biographical Dictionary: People of All Times and Places Who Have Been Important to the History and Life of the State. New York: Somerset Publishers, 1993.

Winona Middle School Media Center Pamphlet File collection of famous Minnesotans.

Electronic

Online Databases (requires subscription):

        DISCovering Collection, Thomson Learning, Gale Group

        InfoTrac Magazine Collection, Thomson Learning, Gale Group

        Junior Reference Collection, Thomson Learning, Gale Group

        Proquest, ProQuest Information and Learning Company

Adobe Photo Deluxe. Macintosh Version 2.0. San Jose: Adobe Systems Incorporated, 1997.

ClarisWorks/AppleWorks. Macintosh Ver 6. Cupertino, California: Apple Computer, 2000.

HyperStudio. Macintosh Ver 3.1 El Cajon, California: Roger Wagner Publishing Company, 1988–1995.

Minnesota Historical Society. 24 July 2002 <http://www.mnhs.org/>.

Type to Learn. Macintosh Networked Version 2.7. Pleasantville, New York: Sunburst Communications Inc., 1997–2000.

"Wabasha Prairie to Winona: Winona's Early History." *Winona County Historical Society*. August 1999. 24 July 2002 <http://www.winona.msus.edu/historicalsociety/sesqui/>.

World Book Online. 27 November 2001 <http://www.worldbookonline.com/>. Requires subscription.

The following resources located on the Winona Public School Web site provide additional information about the Capstone Project:

- Anderson, Mary Alice, ed. "Winona's Cultural History: The Changing Demographics of the Winona Area." Winona Middle School, 1996–2002, a Web site about some of the ethnic groups that settled Winona.
- "Minnesota Resources," Winona Middle School Curriculum Links for 6th grade social studies.
- Technology Help Sheets" (directions used by students to complete portions of the Capstone Project).
- "Managing Resources Capstone Project," a Web site about the project.

To locate the above resources go to the Winona Middle School Web site, <http://www.winona.k12.mn.us/wms> and navigate to the "Media Center and Technology" and "Academic" portions of the Web site. Online versions of some articles can be found on Mary Alice Anderson's home page, located in the staff pages section of the Winona Middle School Web site.

    If you cannot find the resources please contact the project coordinator at *Maryalice@winona.k12.mn.us*.

Equipment

Scanners

Digital camera

Video projector

Scan converters

Server for storage space

Product or Culminating Activity:

Individual components involve creating a product. These are:

Task 1. (D-1, Sixth grade Social Studies) Students research a famous Minnesotan and create a multimedia presentation using *HyperStudio*.

Task 2. (D-3, Sixth grade Language Arts) Word processing documents are written to persuade.

Task 3. (D-3, Eighth grade Communications Technology) Students work in teams to take their pictures using a digital camera. They use *Adobe Photo Deluxe* to further digitize the image by creating an Asian postcard to complete this industrial technology project.

Task 4. (D-3, Eighth grade Communications Technology) Students compile their work in a *HyperStudio* portfolio.

Task 5. (D-2, D-3, Sixth Grade Science) Students gather data about electrical use in a project called Meter Monitor. They present their data in a spreadsheet and chart.

Task 6. (D-3, Seventh grade Social Studies) Students gather statistical information about western European countries and create a database and multiple reports.

Task 7. (D-3, Sixth grade Communications) Students complete a series of keyboarding lessons and write a reflection of their progress.

Assessment Overview: Students are assessed on each component of the Capstone Project as it is completed. The final portfolio is the only component that is both assessed and reported as a State Graduation Preparatory Standard.

Implementation Note: The 2001–2002 school year was the fourth year of project implementation; the 350+ eighth grade students who completed portfolios in spring 2001 were the first to complete the entire project. Most students had the needed files in the server space; we allowed substitutions for students whose files had been lost or who were not attending our school at the time some tasks were complete. All students completed the portfolio. The assessment checklists and record keeping have been streamlined from the initial development in order to facilitate the project without extensive paperwork. However, the checklists are a planning guide and reminder of what we need to teach. Implementing a project that involves more than 1,000 students and 12 teachers is a huge task, but it works well. All students are completing the required components. The language of the standard and the tasks allow for flexibility and evolution as technology changes.

Adaptations and Extensions: We hope that students will chose to include other examples of technology expertise in their final portfolios.

Figure 4.13   Capstone Project

Task 1: Feedback Checklist for Famous Minnesotans Project

Student   **Teacher**

_____   Student selects an appropriate topic.   _____

_____   Student looks in at least two appropriate sources such as Spectrum, online   _____
magazine databases, online encyclopedias and other appropriate sources.

_____   Student takes accurate notes.   _____

_____   Student records sources used according to teacher directions.   _____

_____   Student creates a multimedia presentation appropriate to the topic.   _____

_____   Student spells all words correctly.   _____

_____   Student uses at least one image.   _____

_____   Student creates buttons that work correctly.   _____

_____   Student uses correct grammar and punctuation.   _____

_____   Student accurately lists sources in the bibliography on the last card.   _____

_____   Student follows and applies appropriate technology use guidelines and ethics.   _____

_____   Student successfully saves the project to the Capstone folder.   _____

_____   Student follows and applies technology guidelines and ethics.   _____

Figure 4.14   Capstone Project

Task 2: Feedback Checklist for Word Processed Document

Student   **Teacher**

_____   Student completes Task #2 of grade 6 Language Arts performance package   _____

_____   Student saves the word processing document into the Capstone folder in the   _____
folder on the server.

Figure 4.15   **Capstone Project**

Task 3: Feedback Checklist for Digitized Self-Image

"Dear Mom, I've been to Asia."

Student		Teacher
_____	Student takes photo with the digital camera and saves it in his server space.	_____
_____	Student cuts his/her picture out of the photo for future use.	_____
_____	Student creates the front and back of a postcard using *ClarisWorks Draw*.	_____
_____	Student searches *World Book Online* to find a picture from Asia and pastes the picture on the front of the postcard.	_____
_____	Student superimposes picture of himself/herself on Asian picture to create a "tourist photo."	_____
	Student completes back of postcard.	
_____	"Stamp" designed with *ClarisWorks Draw*;	_____
_____	"Dear Mom or Dad" note explaining the Asian scene.	_____
_____	Student prints front and back of postcard.	_____
_____	Student turns in handwritten notes from *World Book Online* and source citation.	_____

Figure 4.16   Capstone Project

Task 4: Feedback Checklist for Final Capstone Portfolio

Complete these items first. Explain each item in the stack and describe what you did and what you learned.

Student   **Teacher**

_____   Introduction card(s).   _____
                  (Introduce yourself and what your portfolio stack is about)

_____   Spreadsheet sample.   _____
                  (Meter monitor spreadsheet and graph from 6th grade science.)
                  Put each on a separate card. (Substitution approved by teacher _____)

_____   Word processing sample.   _____
                  (Sixth grade language arts writing sample, persuasive or technical writing)

_____   Research example.   _____
                  (Link to sixth grade Famous Minnesotan Social Studies stack)
                  (Substitution approved by teacher _____)

_____   Database card.   _____
                  (Seventh grade Social Studies countries database)
                  (Substitution approved by teacher _____)

_____   Digitized self-image.   _____
                  (Eighth grade Industrial Technology, no substitutions accepted)

_____   Conclusion/Reflection Slide(s).   _____
                  Describe what you've learned by using technology at WMS.

_____   Table of contents card with buttons that provide links to the entire stack.   _____

Complete these items after the above are completed.

_____   Buttons that provide navigation through the stack and to the home card.   _____

_____   Appropriate special effects (transitions, sound).   _____

Optional

_____   Button to link to another *HyperStudio* stack or *PowerPoint* presentation.   _____

_____   Cards that include samples of your technology projects at WMS.   _____
                  (Suggestions: *Adobe Photo Deluxe* pictures, economics projects, other writing samples)

Additional special effects

_____   (Video, animations. Add only after other work is completed)   _____

Overall Comments:

Figure 4.17   **Capstone Project**

Task 5: Feedback Checklist for Meters and Machines

Student   **Teacher**

_____   Student locates his/her electric meter.   _____

_____   Student reads and records meter results daily.   _____

_____   Student records information neatly.   _____

_____   Student takes accurate meter readings for two weeks.   _____

_____   Student subtracts and calculates accurate kilowatt usage.   _____

_____   Student records high and low temperatures.   _____

Overall Comments:

Figure 4.18   **Capstone Project**

Task 6: Feedback Checklist for Database

Student   **Teacher**

_____   Student correctly selects countries.   _____

_____   Student correctly gathers data.   _____

_____   Student correctly selects categories/fields.   _____

_____   Student correctly creates database and fields.   _____

_____   Student correctly records data.   _____

_____   Student correctly uses find function.   _____

_____   Student correctly uses sort function.   _____

Overall Comments:

Figure 4.19 Capstone Project

Task 7: Feedback Checklist for Keyboarding

Student   **Teacher**

_____   Student uses appropriate and safe posture.   _____

_____   Student uses appropriate home row and safe hand position.   _____

_____   Student uses touch typing techniques.   _____

_____   Student memorizes the keyboard.   _____

_____   Student uses appropriate keys.   _____

_____   Student uses the mouse efficiently.   _____

_____   Student keyboarding speed is at or above _____ w.p.m.   _____

_____   Student accuracy is at or above _____ %.   _____

_____   Student sample is stored in Capstone folder.   _____

Figure 4.20   **Capstone Project**

Portfolio Assessment Rubric

Content	1 Poor	2 Fair	3 Good	4 Very Good	Comment
	None or very little of the required content is included.	Some of the required content is included.	All but one of the required content items is included.	All required content is included.	
Mechanics	1 Poor The stack functions poorly, buttons don't work. There are spelling errors.	2 Fair The stack partially functions. Some buttons work. There are spelling errors.	3 Good Most of the stack functions properly. Most buttons work. There are no more than 2 spelling errors.	4 Very Good The entire stack functions properly and all of the buttons work. There are no spelling errors.	Comment
Appearance & Design	1 Poor The stack appears messy and unorganized. There are many colors and little attempt at consistency.	2 Fair The stack shows some attempt of organization and consistency. Colors, designs and effects are somewhat appropriate. Text may be difficult to read.	3 Good Most of the stack is consistent. Most colors, designs, and effects are appropriate. Some text may be difficult to read.	4 Very Good There is consistency in design and color throughout the stack. Colors and backgrounds are pleasing. The text is easy to read.	Comment

Civil War Silhouettes

Carol W. Heinsdorf, Librarian

Julie Buschel, Social Studies Coordinator/Eighth Grade Special Education Teacher

Roxanne Wright, Music Teacher

Rebecca Casiano, Supportive Service Assistant

Roberto Clemente Middle School

122 West Erie Avenue, Philadelphia, Pennsylvania 19140

215-291-5400

cheinsdo@phila.k12.pa.us

Grade Level: 8

Unit Overview: While studying the American Civil War, selected students of varied academic abilities research print and electronic sources for primary and secondary biographical information about both famous and ordinary persons who experienced the war. Each student composes and rehearses a two-to-three minute script portraying his/her character. The students are then videotaped, one after another, speaking as if they were these characters, creating "Civil War Silhouettes." Singing of Negro spirituals accompanies the introduction and closing credits.

Time Frame: Approximately eight weeks

Content Area Standards: School District of Philadelphia Curriculum Frameworks
<http://www.phila.k12.pa.us/teachers/frameworks/grid/gridmast.htm>

Grade 8 Social Studies
Standard 2: Time, Continuity, and Change—Analyze historical events, conditions, trends and issues to understand the way human beings view themselves, their institutions and others, now and over time, to enable them to make informed choices and decisions.
2:3 Demonstrate an understanding that historical events can be interpreted through multiple perspectives.

Standard 4: Individuals, Groups, and Institutions—Demonstrate an understanding of the role of individuals, groups, and institutions and how their actions and interactions exert powerful influences on society.
4:1 Demonstrate an understanding of concepts such as role, status, and social class in describing the interactions of individuals and social groups.

Grade 8 Reading
Standard 1: Apply effective reading strategies to comprehend, organize, analyze, synthesize, and evaluate texts to construct meaning.
1:1 Connect contents, facts, and ideas with own background knowledge and experience.

Grade 8 Writing

Standard 4: Conduct and document inquiry-based research using oral, print, and communications systems.

4:3 Connect prior knowledge to new situations.

Grade 8 Speaking

Standard 2: Speak using effective communication skills including enunciation, inflection, volume, fluency, and non-verbal gestures.

2:1 Speak clearly and audibly.

2:5 Vary voice tone and rate.

Grade 8 Music

Standard 1: Sing a varied repertoire of music alone and with others.

1:1 Sing on pitch and in rhythm with appropriate timbre, text, diction, and posture, maintaining a steady tempo.

Information Power Information Literacy Standards and Indicators: 1.1, 1.4, 2.4, 3.1, 3.4, 7.1, 9.1, 9.2

Cooperative Teaching Plan:

Librarian Will:

- Define topic and determine scope of project, and introduce the topic and project (with teacher).
- Teach and review research methodology from both print and electronic sources including keyword and Boolean searching, selection criteria, use of electronic bookmarks, and noting of print and electronic citations.
- Provide access to print and electronic resources.
- Assist students with research, note taking, and script composition.
- Phrase scripts and supervise slow and clear speech rehearsal.
- Supervise appropriate costuming and hair styling.
- Prepare the staging area.
- Conduct a dress rehearsal, with help from the library assistant.
- Film the videotape, with help from the library assistant.

Social Studies/Special Education Teacher Will:

- Define topic and determine scope of project, and introduce the topic and project (with librarian).
- Teach background information (American Civil War).
- Assist students in selecting persons to research.
- Select students of varied academic abilities to research and portray the identified roles.
- Release actor students to research their characters and compose scripts using print and electronic resources in the IMC/Library.
- Supervise script support. Actors copy scripts to chart paper, from which they will read during taping. Students with special needs memorize scripts from audiotapes prepared by the teacher.
- Rehearse students using slow and clear speech.
- Show the video in the classroom as a culminating product of American Civil War unit.

Music Teacher Will:
- Select soloists.
- Teach and rehearse the singing of Negro spirituals.
- Conduct singers during taping.

Resources:

Print

Afro-American Encyclopedia. North Miami, Florida: Educational Book Publishers, 1974.
The American Civil War A Multicultural Encyclopedia. 7 vol. Danbury, Connecticut: Grolier, 1994.
Hakim, Joy. *War, Terrible War*. New York: Oxford University Press, 1994.

Electronic

"Civil War Women: Primary Sources on the Web." *Sallie Bingham Center for Women's History and Culture in the Rare Book, Manuscript, and Special Collections Library at Duke University*. June 1996. 24 July 2002
    <http://scriptorium.lib.duke.edu/women/cwdocs.html>.
"Excerpts from Slave Narratives, Edited by Steven Mintz." *History at the University of Houston*. 24 July 2002 <http://vi.uh.edu/pages/mintz/primary.htm>.
"Frederick Douglass 'Abolitionist/Editor': A Biography of the Life of Frederick Douglass by Sandra Thomas." *University of Rochester, Department of History*. 24 July 2002
    <http://www.history.rochester.edu/class/douglass/HOME.html>.
"Records of the 105th U.S. Colored Troops." *Civil War@Charleston*. 24 July 2002
    <http://www.awod.com/gallery/probono/cwchas/usct105.html>.
"Scartoons: Racial Satire and the Civil War." *American Studies at the University of Virginia*. 24 July 2002 <http://xroads.virginia.edu/~CAP/SCARTOONS/cartoons.html>.
"Slave Narratives. 1936–1938." *University of Missouri-St. Louis, Thomas Jefferson Library, Reference Department*. 24 July 2002
    <http://www.umsl.edu/~libweb/blackstudies/moslave.htm>.
"The Valley of the Shadow: Two Communities in the American Civil War." *The Institute for Advanced Technology in the Humanities*. 24 July 2002
    <http://jefferson.village.Virginia.edu/vshadow2/>.

Equipment and Supplies

Tape recorder and player
Chart paper and markers to copy scripts in large print for reading while being videotaped
Display board for posting script to be read as character is videotaped
Costumes (from the waist up, only)
Overhead projector (optional)
Video camera with blank videotape and tripod
TV/VCR for cueing tape

Product or Culminating Activity: A 20-minute video, "Civil War Silhouettes," in which Harriet Tubman, John Brown the abolitionist, John Brown, a slave, Johnny Clem, an underage Union soldier, Johnny Bravo, a Confederate soldier, and Clara Barton all speak in cameo appearances. The introduction and credits are accompanied by the voices of students singing Negro spirituals.

Assessment Overview: Assessment takes place throughout the project. Students selected to perform, including those with special learning needs, must give a performance of which they can be proud. Therefore, research for content, script composition, and rehearsals are constantly evaluated by both the librarian and classroom teacher, so that the final video performance relays accurate information in cogent, compelling, first-person narratives. Script is assessed using the Pennsylvania Writing Assessment Holistic Scoring Guide. Please see <http://www.temple.edu/CETP/temple_teach/ PA-Write.htm>.

Adaptations and Extensions: A student who had had reconstructive facial surgery requested that he not be seen on the videotape. An overhead projector was used to cast his shadow, which was videotaped, instead. This was particularly appropriate because he portrayed the part of a slave, for whom no photographic image would be available. Modifications to the general curriculum were made for those students with special needs included in the regular education classroom, utilizing various cooperative learning strategies. For example, text was read aloud to students with special needs who were then able to respond orally to the written assignment or audio record their responses.

Students brought in food typical of a Civil War soldier's rations as an extension, and students with special needs created an illustrated "ABC" book of the Civil War.

Figure 4.21   **Civil War Silhouettes**

Project Planner

ESSENTIAL QUESTION (What I am studying):

MY QUESTIONS (What I want to find out based on my essential question):

KEYWORDS ("Look-up" words that will lead me to good information):

ELECTRONIC RESOURCES/URLS (Internet addresses where someone else could find the information I found):

PRINT RESOURCES (Books in which someone else could find the information I found):

The sample below is based upon the life of Clara Barton.

ESSENTIAL QUESTION:
> How did Clara Barton affect history?

MY QUESTIONS:
> Who is Clara Barton?
> What did she do during the American Civil War?

KEYWORDS:

Print resources:	Barton, Clara	Electronic resources:	"Clara Barton"
	Red Cross		"American Red Cross"
			"Red Cross"

ELECTRONIC RESOURCES/URLs:
"American Treasures of the Library of Congress Memory: Clara Barton." 28 June 2002.
> 24 July 2002 <http://lcweb.loc.gov/exhibits/treasures/trm072.html>.

PRINT RESOURCES:
"Barton, Clara." *The American Civil War A Multicultural Encyclopedia*. Danbury,
> Connecticut: Grolier, 1994.

Figure 4.22   **Civil War Silhouettes**

Script Planner

Note to the Student: Please incorporate the following items into your script.

- Biographical information about my character—birth and death dates, education, family, jobs held, places lived, awards received, etc.

- An interesting personal story about my character

- A quote from my character

Figure 4.23 **Civil War Silhouettes**

Production Planner

Note to Students Singing: The music teacher will select the Negro spirituals and rehearse you independently of the following schedule, in preparation for the final production date.

WEEKS 1–3 — Research
Answer "MY QUESTIONS" using the Project Planner.

WEEK 4 — Script Writing
Write the first draft of the script from research notes, using the Script Planner. Choose one of two formats for the script.

1. Journal/diary entry for a day or two (good for telling about special events). It should include:
   - Setting (Where is this taking place? Year, season, weather if important).
   - Character's relationship to the people and places around him/her.
   - A description of the events happening around him/her.
   - The character's observations and feelings about those events.
2. Autobiography, looking back on the character's life (good for telling about motivation, why the character did what he/she did).

The script is limited to two handwritten pages, or one typed page. It can be shorter.

WEEKS 5–6 — Re-write Scripts
Refine and re-write your script as we discuss costumes and gather appropriate pieces of clothing.

WEEK 7 — Production Preparation
Copy script in large letters onto chart paper. Add phrasing marks (slashes between groups of words). Rehearse using slow and clear speech. Have costume checked and agree upon an appropriate hairstyle. Singers will rehearse. Type the title page, casting, and credits in preparation for filming. Select a plain wall with access to electrical plugs as the staging area for filming.

WEEK 8 — Video Production
Prepare the camera to videotape "silhouettes" by using a paper punch to make a hole in black paper. This paper is fitted and taped over the lens of the camera, giving a keyhole appearance to the image. Arrange the staging area, chair or stool, display board with tape for posting scripts, TV/VCR for cueing, and video camera with videotape and tripod. Film test shots.

Film the title page with students' voices heard singing in the background. (This may be videotaped in a location different from the characters' staging area.) Students portraying characters are videotaped individually. They appear in profile from the shoulders up against the plain background, without props, reading their scripts, which are posted out of sight of the video camera. The video is completed with filming of the cast list and credits, again with the voices of students heard in the background singing Negro spirituals.

Figure 4.24 **Civil War Silhouettes**

Video Assessment Guidelines

Note to Teacher: These Guidelines/Questions may be used as a rubric.

Note to Student: Because your performance must be one of which you can be proud, both you and your teachers must be sure that all the questions listed below can be answered with a "Yes" BEFORE your final videotaping.

CONTENT

Teacher		**Student**
_____	Is the information included factually accurate?	_____
_____	Is the character's significance in the American Civil War setting described clearly?	_____
_____	Does the narrative relate personal information about the character?	_____
_____	Is the script well organized and coherent?	_____

PERFORMANCE

_____	Is speech clear, audible, and delivered with inflection?	_____
_____	Are costumes and hairstyles appropriate to the period?	_____
_____	Is the singing on pitch and the words clearly articulated?	_____
_____	Does the singing conform to the conductor's directions?	_____

Creating A Utopian Society

Linda C. Thomas, Media Specialist
John Pierce, Core Teacher, Eighth Grade Reading, Language, History
Barnard White Middle School
725 Whipple Road
Union City, California, 94587
510-471-5363 x 6001
Linda_Thomas@nhusd.k12.ca.us

Grade Level: 8

Unit Overview: In Creating a Utopian Society, students read literature to discover how utopian societies have been portrayed and then research historical utopian societies. After brainstorming and listing the inadequacies of existing society, students set forth a model of an "ideal" society and discuss the societal components necessary to achieve it, including the desirable character traits of citizens, governmental constructs, and economic base necessary to the society. Students discuss methods of encouraging citizens to behave in ways that will benefit the ideal society and accommodate societal mores such as promoting conservation and treating everyone equally. The unit culminates with the creation of a literary anthology with a utopian theme.

Time Frame: A minimum of 10 weeks or a maximum of a semester.

Content Area Standards: Content Standards for California Public Schools
<http://www.cde.ca.gov/standards/>

Language Arts, Grade 8
Reading
2.0 Reading Comprehension (Focus on Informational Materials)
Students read and understand grade level appropriate material. They describe and connect the essential ideas, arguments, and perspectives of the text by using their knowledge of text structure, organization, and purpose.
Comprehension and Analysis of Grade-Level Appropriate Text
2.3 Find similarities and differences between texts in the treatment, scope, or organization of ideas.

3.0 Literary Response and Analysis
Students read and respond to historically or culturally significant works of literature that reflect and enhance their studies of history and social science. They clarify the ideas and connect them to other literary works.
Narrative Analysis of Grade-Level-Appropriate Text
3.3. Compare and contrast motivations and reactions of literary characters from different historical eras confronting similar situations or conflicts.

3.5 Identify and analyze recurring themes (e.g., good versus evil) across traditional and contemporary works.

Writing
1.0 Writing Strategies
Students write clear, coherent, and focused essays. The writing exhibits students' awareness of audience and purpose. Essays contain formal introductions, supporting evidence, and conclusions. Student's progress through the stages of the writing process as needed.

Organization and Focus
1.1 Create compositions that establish a controlling impression, have a coherent thesis, and end with a clear and well-supported conclusion.
1.2 Establish coherence within and among paragraphs through effective transitions, parallel structures, and similar writing techniques.
1.3 Support theses or conclusions with analogies, paraphrases, quotations, opinions, authorities, comparison, and similar devices

Research and Technology
1.4 Plan and conduct multiple-step information searches by using computer networks and modems.
1.5 Achieve an effective balance between researched information and original ideas.

Evaluation and Revision
1.6 Revise writing for word choice; appropriate organization, consistent point of view; and transitions between paragraphs, passages, and ideas.

Written and Oral English Language Conventions
1.0 Written and Oral English Language Conventions
Students write and speak with a command of Standard English conventions appropriate to this grade level.

Sentence Structure
1.1 Use correct and varied sentence types and sentence openings to present a lively and effective personal style.
Grammar
1.4 Edit written manuscripts to ensure that correct grammar is used.
Punctuation and Capitalization
1.5 Use correct punctuation and capitalization.

2.0 Writing Applications (Genres and Their Characteristics)
Students write narrative, expository, persuasive, and descriptive essays of at least 500 to 700 words in each genre. Student writing demonstrates a command of standard American English and the research, organizational, and drafting strategies outlined in Writing Standard 1.0

Using the writing strategies of grade eight outlined in Writing Standard 1.0, students:

2.2 Write responses to literature:
   a. Exhibit careful reading and insight in their interpretations.
   b. Connect the student's own responses to the writer's techniques and to specific textual references.

c. Draw supported inferences about the effects of a literary work on its audience.

d. Support judgments through references to the text, other works, other authors, or to personal knowledge.

History-Social Science Standards, Grade 8
United States History and Geography: Growth and Conflict

8.1 Students understand the major events preceding the founding of the nation and relate their significance to the development of American constitutional democracy.

8.1.2. Analyze the philosophy of government expressed in the Declaration of Independence, with an emphasis on government as a means of securing individual rights (e.g., key phrases such as "all men are created equal, that they are endowed by their Creator with certain inalienable rights.")

8.2 Students analyze the political principles underlying the U.S. Constitution and compare the enumerated and implied powers of the federal government.

8.2.6. Enumerate the powers of government set forth in the Constitution and the fundamental liberties ensured by the Bill of Rights.

Content Area Standards: SCORE (Schools of California Online Resources for Education) History and Social Science Analysis Skills <http://score.rims.k12.ca.us/critical_thinking/research.html>

History-Social Science Thinking and Analysis Skills, Grades 6 through 8

In addition to the standards for grades six through eight, students demonstrate the following intellectual reasoning, reflection, and research skills:

Historical Research, Evidence, and Point of View

1. Students frame questions that can be answered by historical study and research.
2. Students distinguish fact from opinion in historical narratives and stories.
3. Students distinguish relevant from irrelevant information, essential from incidental information, and verifiable from unverifiable information in historical narratives and stories.

Historical Interpretation

1. Students explain the central issues and problems from the past, placing people and events in a matrix of time and place.

Information Power Information Literacy Standards and Indicators: 1.3, 1.4, 1.5, 2.1, 2.2, 2.3, 2.4, 3.1, 3.2, 3.3, 3.4, 5.1, 5.2, 5.3, 6.1, 6.2, 7.1, 8.1, 8.2, 8.3, 9.1, 9.2, 9.3, 9.4

Cooperative Teaching Plan:

Media Specialist Will:

- Introduce project with a discussion of the origin and development of utopias, beginning with Sir Thomas More's *Utopia* in the 1500s, and including positive and negative utopias in literature and history such as the hippie communes of the 1960s, the Nazi regime of the 1940s and the Shaker religious communities of the 1700s.
- Facilitate brainstorming among students to determine current societal characteristics and identify necessary changes needed to improve and or reconstruct society in the future.
- Assist in student selection of utopian literature and review essays of utopian thought.

- Oversee weekly student-facilitated discussions of elements of positive and negative utopian societies in weekly assigned chapters.
- Teach students to locate and evaluate Internet sources.
- Supervise student research of utopian Web sites and location of sources that describe early utopian communities in American history such as the Shakers.
- Teach students to operate the Camera Man unit.
- Supervise videotaping of weekly seminars using the "Synergy System" closed circuit TV system and make tapes available for class and teacher viewing
- In collaboration with the teacher, assesses the written product using the rubric.

Teacher Will:
- Plan and collaborate with the media specialist to determine the relevant connections between the utopia project and the classroom curriculum.
- Explain the overall unit to the students, providing objectives, timelines, and expectations.
- Discuss historical utopias in American society within the context of whole class instruction (i.e., the Shakers).
- Release students for weekly seminars in the Media Center.
- Periodically meet with the media specialist to discuss the seminar and student responses.
- In collaboration with the media specialist, assesses the written product using the rubric.

Resources:
Print
Haddix, Margaret Peterson. *Running Out of Time*. New York: Simon & Schuster, 1995.
Lowry, Lois. *The Giver*. New York: Houghton Mifflin, 1993.
Orwell, George. *Animal Farm: A Fairy Story*. New York: New American Library, 1959.
Orwell, George. *Nineteen Eighty-Four*. New York: New American Library, 1961.
Streissguth, Thomas. *Utopian Visionaries*. Minneapolis: Oliver Press, 1999.

Electronic
Targowski, Henry W. "Utopia." *Mark-Space*. 24 July 2002
        <http://www.euro.net/mark-space/glosUtopia.html>.
"Utopia" *The New York Public Library*. 24 July, 2002
        <http://www.nypl.org/utopia/Pt3resources.html>.
Utopia on the Internet. 24 July, 2002 <http://users.erols.com/jonwill/utopialist.htm>.

Equipment
Video cameras and/or Camera Man units.

Product or Culminating Activity: Students create a literary anthology that incorporates their differing views and personal beliefs about the creation of a utopian society through satire, poetry, essays, or short stories. Each written piece is submitted as an entry in the school and district annual Young Author Faire. Students also share excerpts from their opus at a parent tea for Young Author Faire winners and discuss the development and resolution of their project with the student and parent audience in small group discussions.

Assessment Overview: Written products to be anthologized and submitted to the Young Author Faire are assessed using a three-point rubric, by the media specialist and the teacher.

| Figure 4.25 | Creating a Utopian Society |

Project Overview

- Answer the following questions from your personal perspective, then discuss with your group before reading a novel or researching past utopian societies:
  1. What are the components of an "ideal society?"
  2. Compare and contrast them with the existing American society. Which elements are present and which are missing? Which changes would you make to improve our current society?
  3. Suppose you were creating an "ideal society" on a Lunar Station. How would you structure it to best reflect your "ideal society?"
     a. What governmental structure would be required? Would you retain the democratic structure of the United States government, the Constitution and the Bill of Rights?
     b. Which would be maintained and which would be eliminated? Are there other governmental structures which you would utilize instead?
     c. What educational methods would be used to develop citizens who were responsive to your view of a desired society?
     d. What would be done with citizens who disagreed with your views?
     e. Would you use genetic engineering or psychological conditioning to guarantee citizens who were supportive of your views? Why or why not?

- Read one of the novels that reflect a positive or negative utopia, and answer the previous questions as they were addressed in each book. Did you agree or disagree with the author's perspective? Explain. Discuss your responses with your group members. Did you agree or disagree with the group consensus?

- Read the remainder of the novels that were selected for this project and repeat the process.

- After completing all of the novels and discussing them with your group members, reassess the original three questions. Did your personal perspective change? Why or why not?

- Research past attempts to create positive or negative utopian societies using print or non-print resources and reassess the original three questions for each of them.

The Shakers-Ann Lee and Joseph Meacham	Brook Farm-George Ripley
The Oneida Community-John Humphrey Noyes	The Third Reich-Adolph Hitler
The Israeli Kibbutzim	The Communes of the 1960s

  Did your personal perspective change? Why or why not?
  Did your group reach consensus on whether each was a utopian society? Why or why not?

- Choose a written format and describe your utopian society in an essay, short story, poetry or other genre. Create a written anthology of the group responses.

Figure 4.26   **Creating a Utopian Society**

Quiz

Answer the following questions on a separate piece of paper. Attach this sheet to your answer sheet.

Five points are possible for each part of a question, for a maximum of 25 points each.

1. What is a utopia? List five aspects of a positive or negative utopia.   _____ Pts

2. Do we live in a utopian society? List five reasons supporting your position.   _____ Pts

3. Describe the utopian society in one of the novels that were read and discussed in your group. What were five important elements of the society that the author included?   _____ Pts

4. Describe an actual utopian society that you researched. What were five important elements of that society?   _____ Pts

Total points out of 100 =   _____ Pts.

Figure 4.27   Creating a Utopian Society

Rubric for Written Evaluation

Each item will be scored from 1 (lowest) to 3 (highest).

Score point 3:	**The writing shows a thorough understanding of the audience and purpose.** • The writing shows thorough topic development. • The writing includes a unique approach to the topic. • The writing shows thorough development of ideas. • The writing incorporates relevant support materials from independent research.
Score point 2:	**The writing shows consistent understanding of the audience and purpose.** • The writing shows consistent topic development. • The writing includes a predictable approach to the topic. • The writing shows consistent development of a few ideas. • The writing incorporates some relevant support materials from independent research.
Score point 1:	**The writing shows inconsistent understanding of the audience and purpose.** • The writing shows minimal topic development. • The writing includes no predictable approach to the topic. • The writing does not demonstrate a change or modification of the author's original views. • The writing does not incorporate relevant support materials from independent research.

Ecological Problem Solving

Maureen S. Irwin, Middle School Librarian

Martha Barss, Seventh Grade Science Teacher, Edie Windsor, Computer Teacher,

Maria Hampton and Louisa Wyskiel, Math Teachers

Roland Park Country School

5204 Roland Avenue, Baltimore, Maryland 21210-1996

410-323-5500

maureen_irwin@rcds.rye.ny.us

Grade Level: 7

Unit Overview: Ecological Problem Solving requires students to examine human impact on the environment by studying ecological problems within a structure similar to real-world scientific inquiry. Each team of 3–4 students will be given a problem to study. At the end of the two-week project period, students will present their findings in the form of a *PowerPoint* project to the other groups in their class. They will also jigsaw during grade level time with other groups who have studied the same problem. At that time, the students will see what other groups, who have studied the same problem, have concluded.

Time Frame: Two weeks (10 class periods)

Content Area Standards: Maryland Science Content Standards, June 6, 2000
<http://www.mdk12.org/share/standards/constds_science.pdf>
Note: MLO refers to Maryland Learning Outcomes

1.0 Skills and Processes. Students will demonstrate the thinking and acting inherent in the practice of science.

1.0 Skills and Processes: Scientific Inquiry

1.8.3 Use observations, research, and select appropriate scientific information to form predictions and hypotheses. (MLO 1.1.3)

1.8.7 Collect, organize, and display data in ways others can verify (i.e. numbers, statistics, tables, graphs, drawings, charts, diagrams) using appropriate instruments (e.g., *calculators, spreadsheets, databases, and graphing programs*). (MLO 1.1.6)

1.8.8 Analyze and summarize data to identify trends and form a logical argument about a cause and effect relationship or a sequence of events. (MLO 1.1.7)

1.8.9 Interpret and communicate findings (i.e., speaking, writing, and drawing) in a form suited to the purpose and audience, using developmentally appropriate methods including technology tools and telecommunications. (MLO 1.1.8)

1.0 Skills and Processes: Critical Thinking

1.8.14 Provide supporting evidence when forming conclusions, devising a plan or solving a practical problem. (MLO 1.2.4)

1.8.15 Analyze and extend patterns. (MLO 1.2.5)

1.8.16 Modify ideas based on new information from developmentally appropriate readings, data, and the ideas of others. (MLO 1.2.6)

1.8.17 Describe to others how scientific information was used. (MLO 1.2.7)

1.8.18 Apply scientific principles and/or concepts to understand a new situation. (MLO 1.3.1)

1.0 Skills and Processes: Applications of Science

1.8.20 Apply concepts and processes of science to take and defend a position relative to an issue. (MLO 1.3.2)

1.8.21 Use the knowledge of science and available scientific equipment to devise a plan to solve a global problem. (MLO 1.3.3)

1.0 Skills and Processes: Technology

1.8.26 Explain that science and technology have strongly influenced life under different technological circumstances in the past and continue to do so today.

Earth/Space Science. Students will use scientific skills and processes to explain the chemical and physical interactions (i.e., natural forces and cycles, transfer of energy) of the environment, Earth, and the universe that occur over time.

2.0 Earth/Space Science: Earth History

2.8.4 Explain the physical processes that produce renewable and nonrenewable natural resources (e.g., fertile soils, fossils, fuels, and timber).

6.0 Environmental Science. Students will use scientific skills and processes to explain the interactions of environmental factors (living and non-living) and analyze their impact from a local to a global perspective.

6.0 Environmental Science: Interdependence of Organisms

6.8.2 Identify and explain the interdependency of organisms within the environment in a given ecosystem (i.e., producer/consumer, predator/prey, host/parasite). (MLO 6.1)

6.12.2 Use physical, chemical, biological, and ecological concepts to analyze and explain the inter-dependence of organisms within the environment.

6.0 Environmental Science: Natural Resources and Human Needs

6.8.4 Compare how different parts of the world have varying amounts and types of natural resources and how the use of those resources determines environmental quality (i.e. soil erosion, water pollution, deforestation).

6.0 Environmental Science: Environmental Issues

6.8.5 Analyze how human activities can accelerate or magnify many naturally occurring changes (i.e., erosion, air and water quality, populations). (MLO 6.2)

6.8.6 Compare different ways of obtaining, transforming, and distributing energy from various sources (e.g., fossil fuels, sun, water, radioisotopes) and their impact on the environment.

Information Power Information Literacy Standards and Indicators: 1.1, 1.2, 1.3, 1.4, 1.5, 2.4, 3.1, 3.2, 3.3, 3.4, 8.2, 8.3, 9.1, 9.3

Cooperative Teaching Plan:

Librarian Will:

■ Introduce the Big6™ process research model by Eisenberg and Berkowitz and guide students in its use for this assignment.

■ Teach navigation of the EPA Web site and help students formulate questions based on their problems.

- Assist with split-screen note taking, cutting and pasting of tables and URLs, and creating bibliographies.
- Provide ecology print references and sources to supplement statistical material.
- Develop note-taking sheets for use with print resources.
- Attend presentation sessions and provide input for final assessments.

Science Teacher Will:
- Lay groundwork for basic understandings in ecological problem solving.
- Develop "problems" to be solved based on information retrievable from EPA Web site and accessible to seventh grade science students.
- Guide students in use of systematic investigative methods.
- Help students to formulate questions.
- Develop time management plan, student and team evaluation sheets, and final assessment rubrics.
- Meet regularly with teams to assess progress.
- Provide final assessment of written material and oral presentation.

Computer Teacher Will:
- Teach presentation software and assist with its use.

Math Teachers Will:
- Assist with graphing and reading of tables.
- Act as advisors for students working with data sets.

Resources

Print
50 Simple Things You Can Do to Save the Earth. Berkeley, California: Earthworks Press, 1989.

The 1994 Information Please Environmental Almanac. New York: Houghton Mifflin, 1993.

Aronson, Elliot. *Nobody Left to Hate*. New York: W. H. Freeman, 2000, pp. 135–145.
  (Consult this resource for a description of the Jigsaw Classroom model.)

Baines, John D. *Keeping the Air Clean*. Austin: Raintree Steck-Vaughn, 1998.

Barss, Karen. *Clean Water*. New York: Chelsea House Publishers, 1992.

DuTemple, Lesley A. *Oil Spills*. San Diego, California: Lucent Books, 1999.

Gay, Kathlyn. *The Greenhouse Effect*. New York: Franklin Watts, 1986.

Gay, Kathlyn. *Water Pollution*. New York: Franklin Watts, 1990.

Harms, Valerie. *The National Audubon Society Almanac of the Environment: The Ecology of Everyday Life*. New York: G. P. Putnam's Sons, 1994.

Herda, D. J. *Environmental America* series. Brookfield, Connecticut: Millbrook Press, 1991.

Kahl, Jonathan D. Hazy Skies: *Weather and the Environment*. Minneapolis: Lerner Publications, 1998.

Kellert, Stephen R., ed. *The Encyclopedia of the Environment*. New York: Macmillan Library Reference USA, ©1997.

Lee, Sally. *The Throwaway Society*. New York: Franklin Watts, 1990.

Managing Planet Earth: Readings from Scientific American Magazine. New York: W. H. Freeman, 1990.

Mason, Robert J. *Atlas of United States Environmental Issues*. New York: Macmillan, 1990.

McLeish, Ewan. *Keeping Water Clean*. Austin: Raintree Steck-Vaughn, 1998.

Middleton, Nick. *Atlas of Environmental Issues*. New York: Facts on File, 1989.

Miller, Christina G. *Air Alert: Rescuing the Earth's Atmosphere*. New York: Atheneum, 1996.

Morrison, Earl et al. *Science Plus*. Level Red: Austin: Holt, Rinehart and Winston, 2002.

O'Connor, Karen. *Garbage*. San Diego: Lucent Books, 1989.

Wroble, Lisa A. *The Ocean*. San Diego : Lucent Books, 1998.

Yount, Lisa. *Our Endangered Planet. Air*. Minneapolis: Lerner Publications, 1995.

Electronic

Online Databases (requires subscription):

> *SIRS Researcher*, SIRS, Mandarin Inc.
>
> *Proquest*, ProQuest Information and Learning Company

Energy Information Administration. 21 June 2002. 24 July 2002
> <http://www.eia.doe.gov/>.

"EPA Student Center." *U.S. Environmental Protection Agency*. 28 June 2002. 24 July 2002
> <http:www.epa.gov/students>.

Microsoft Excel 2002. Redmond, Washington: Microsoft Corporation, 2002.

Microsoft Word 2002. Redmond, Washington: Microsoft Corporation, 2002.

Microsoft PowerPoint 2002. Redmond, Washington: Microsoft Corporation, 2002.

"Statistical Abstract of the United States." *U.S. Census Bureau*. 1 February 2001. 24 July 2002
> <http://www.census.gov/prod/www/statistical-abstract-us.html>.

USA Geograph. CD-ROM. Minneapolis: MECC, 1993.

Product or Culminating Activity: A *PowerPoint* presentation detailing findings and recommendations of the team, including two tables and two graphs. At least one graph must be a scatter plot, showing a correlation or non-correlation between two numerical datasets from *USA Geograph*. Tables, graphs, and written explanations of data results are viewed and approved by a seventh grade math teacher before inclusion in the final presentation. A correctly formatted bibliography, including all resources used in the project, must be included in the presentation.

Assessment Overview: During the two-week period, each student must maintain a portfolio including assignment sheets and notes to be checked by the science teacher. Science teacher and librarian assess *PowerPoint* presentation using rubrics found on Presentation Score Guide. Classmates assess presentations with the Student Evaluation.

| Figure 4.28 | Ecological Problem Solving |

Student Overview

Overview: Each team of 3–4 students will be given one of the following problems to study during the two-week project period. On the final two days of the project period, students will present their findings in the form of a *PowerPoint* project to the other groups in their class. They will also jigsaw during grade level time on the final day with other groups who have studied the same problem. At that time, students will see what other groups, who have studied the same problem, have concluded.

Resources: *USA Geograph*
                   Microsoft Excel
                   PowerPoint
                   Library print and electronic resources
                   Science textbook

Human resources: All 7th grade scientists
                   Science Teacher
                   Librarian
                   Math Teachers
                   Computer Teacher

Project Requirements:

1. At first, students will work together to decide what they need to find out through research to answer the questions asked. They will divide up the research tasks among the members of the group, and each person on the team should have a research question to investigate. Research will be done both on *USA Geograph* and in the library print and electronic resources. Both the librarian and the computer teacher will serve as advisors during the research phase of the project.
2. Teams will meet with the science teacher at two times during the project period to discuss how the team's research is progressing and any problems the team is having in working together effectively. All teams must arrange a time with the science teacher by signing up on the schedule. All members of the team must be present at these meeting. Points will be added to the group grade for attending the meetings.
3. Students must include two tables and two graphs in their *PowerPoint* presentation. At least one of the graphs must be a scatter plot and show a correlation or non-correlation between two numerical data sets from *USA Geograph*. Tables, graphs, and written explanations of what the data show must be viewed and approved by a seventh grade math teacher before they can be included in a final *PowerPoint* presentation.
4. A bibliography including all resources used in studying the project must be included in the *PowerPoint* presentation. Correct format must be used for each entry. The bibliography must be viewed and approved by the science teacher or the librarian before it is included in a final *PowerPoint* presentation.
5. A guide sheet will outline the requirements for the *PowerPoint* presentation. The presentation will be graded based on these requirements. The grade for the presentation will be counted as a group grade and will be out of 100 points.

Figure 4.28   **(continued from page 93)**

Ecological Problems: Each team will be assigned a problem.

1. Coal burning has been associated with a number of environmental problems. What is the likely impact economically, socially and environmentally of restricting the burning of coal in the northeastern region of the USA during the next two decades? Why would it be desirable to implement such restrictions?

2. Many scientists have predicted a period of major climactic change in the future. Predict the economic and environmental impact on the northeastern region of the USA of a dramatic change in climate due to the alleged Greenhouse Effect. What could be done now to reduce the chances of such a climactic change?

3. You are a major industrialist who has just learned about sustainable development. You want to set up a new factory that is environmentally sensitive because it uses local renewable resources for raw materials, uses renewable energy sources, and does not pollute the ample clean water and air that is present in the area. You want to build it in a state that has a low risk of natural hazards, a high unemployment rate and a low toxic emission rate. In what state will you build your factory? What will you manufacture? What local raw materials and energy sources will you use? How will you protect the clean air and water that is present today?

4. You are an environmental chemist who has just obtained a grant to study the effect of acid rain on farm crops. You have a budget of $5,000 for travel expenses, and you estimate that it will cost you approximately $1,000 in travel and hotel costs for each state you visit. Plan your trip to five states to conduct first-hand research on the problem. Support your decision to go to each state with data. Explain what kind of research you want to do when you get to each state. Finally, propose ways to minimize the impact of acid rain on the agricultural production of these states.

5. You are an environmental chemist who has just obtained a grant to study the possible effects of soil erosion on the value of the agricultural production in a state. You have a budget of $5,000 for travel expenses and you estimate that it will cost you approximately $1,000 in travel and hotel costs for each state you visit. Plan your trip to five states to conduct first-hand research on the problem. Support your decision to go to each state with data. Explain what kind of research you want to do when you get to each state. Finally, propose ways to minimize the impact of soil erosion on the agricultural economy of these states.

Figure 4.29 **Ecological Problem Solving**

Time Management Plan

Name _____

Date	Class Activity	Homework
(Day 1)	Introduction to project requirements New group brainstorming about problem Research skills with librarian Acid Rain Quiz	Challenge Your Thinking pp. 64–65 Questions 2, 3, and 5 only Use IPQ and be thorough in your answers. 5 points per question
(Day 2)	Research Day—Mac lab and library available	
(Day 3)	Research—Mac lab and library available	
Day 4)	Research—Mac lab and library available Sign up for your mid-project group meeting with the science teacher	
(Day 5)	Start work on *PowerPoint* presentation in PC lab Laptop available with *USA Geograph*, if needed	

Figure 4.29   **(continued from page 95)**

Date	Class Activity	Homework
(Day 6)	Work on *PowerPoint* presentation in PC lab	
(Day 7)	Work on *PowerPoint* presentation in PC lab	
(Day 8)	Work on *PowerPoint* presentation in PC lab	
(Day 9)		
(Day 10)	7-1, 7-2, 7-3 present projects in class All projects presented a second time at grade level	Portfolios due next class. Be sure that you have followed the guide sheet

Figure 4.30   Ecological Problem Solving

Individual Research Notes

Must be in Portfolio: Start a new sheet when you start to research a new question

Name _____

Research Question: _____
_____

Keywords: _____

Bibliographic Entry: _____
_____

Notes (No sentences!)

Signature of Approval: _____

Bibliographic Entry: _____
_____

Notes (No sentences!)

Signature of Approval: _____

Figure 4.31   **Ecological Problem Solving**

Student Evaluation

Title of Presentation: _____

Rating	1	2	3	4	5	6	7	8	9	10
	Poor									Excellent

What I Liked Best:

_____

_____

Needs Improvement:

_____

_____

•••

Title of Presentation: _____

Rating	1	2	3	4	5	6	7	8	9	10
	Poor									Excellent

What I Liked Best:

_____

_____

Needs Improvement:

_____

_____

•••

Title of Presentation: _____

Rating	1	2	3	4	5	6	7	8	9	10
	Poor									Excellent

What I Liked Best:

_____

_____

Needs Improvement:

_____

_____

| Figure 4.32 | Ecological Problem Solving |

Presentation Score Guide

Team Members: _____

Requirements	Points Possible	Points Earned
Title Slide: attracts attention of audience to the problem being presented	5	
Causes: accurately explained using slides to enhance script	15	
Effects: accurately explained using slides to enhance script	15	
Solutions: accurately explained using slides to enhance script	15	
Graphs: correctly used to explain a cause, effect or solution	15	
Closing Slide: summarizes problem and what people can do to reduce the problem	5	
Handout: accurately explains the problem and possible solutions in language that is easily understood	15	
Timing: the presentation was well-scripted and presented smoothly with all members of the team involved	5	
Background and Transitions: enhance the presentation and transition smoothly	5	
Spelling and Grammar: correct on all slides	5	
Total	100	

Figure 4.33 **Ecological Problem Solving**

Team Evaluation

Team Members: _____

Topic: _____

Category and Comments	Points Possible	Points Earned
Team Meetings/Self-Evaluation	**10**	
Time	**10**	
PowerPoint **Presentation**	**70**	
Quiz Results	**10**	
TEAM GRADE FOR PROJECT	**100**	

An Era in Time
Nancy Larimer, Library Media Specialist
Nikki Menard, Tenth Grade English Teacher
Lincoln Northeast High School
2635 N. 63rd Street, Lincoln, Nebraska 68507
402-436-1340
nlarimer@lps.org

Grade Level: 10 (Students are part of a "school within a school" program designed for those who are deficient in credits for graduation, serious about receiving a high school diploma, and not receiving special education services.)

Unit Overview: During An Era in Time, an interdisciplinary English unit, students immerse themselves in a particular culture during a specific period in history. Following pre-reading activities such as guest speakers and films, students examine connections among the arts, music, science, people, places, and events in a wide variety of resources, including reference books, nonfiction, fiction, biographies, poetry, drama, film, children's literature, music, dance, and local museums. Following an introduction to information literacy skills, students undertake research in the library media center. As they read, students journal questions and responses, as well as any problems they may encounter. A facsimile newspaper and oral presentation by each student are the culminating products.

Time Frame: Three weeks. Students work in the library media center for approximately one week of that time.

Content Area Standards: Lincoln Public Schools State Standards, Lincoln, Nebraska (based on Nebraska Department of Education Reading/Writing Standards—Grade 12) <http://www.nde.state.ne.us/READ/Standards/ReadingWritingStandards.htm>

Reading/Writing/Speaking/Listening Standards (Grade 12)
12.1. Reading
12.1.1 By the end of the twelfth grade, students will identify the basic facts and essential ideas in what they have read or viewed.

12.1.2 By the end of twelfth grade, students will locate, access, and evaluate resources to identify appropriate information.

12.1.6 By the end of the twelfth grade, students will identify and analyze the structure, elements, stylistic devices and meaning/purpose of nonfiction or informational material and provide evidence from the text to support their understanding.

12.2 Writing
12.2.1 By the end of the twelfth grade, students will identify and apply knowledge of the structure of the English language and standard English conventions for sentence structure, usage, punctuation, capitalization, and spelling.

12.2.2 By the end of the twelfth grade, students will apply a process to develop and improve written texts as appropriate to the intended purpose, audience, and form.

12.2.3 By the end of the twelfth grade, students will produce varied written texts which communicate effectively in expository and narrative prose.

12.2.4 By the end of the twelfth grade, students will use creative and critical thinking strategies and skills to generate original and meaningful products.

12.3 Speaking

12.3.1 By the end of the twelfth grade, students will pose questions and contribute their own information or ideas in group discussions.

12.3.2 By the end of the twelfth grade, students will make oral presentations/public addresses that demonstrate appropriate consideration of audience, purpose, and information to be conveyed.

12.4 Listening

12.4.1 By the end of the twelfth grade, students will use listening skills for a variety of purposes.

The Nebraska Social Studies/History Standards, Grade 12
http://www.nde.state.ne.us

12.1 World History: 1000 A.D. to the Present

12.1.10 Students will analyze major 20th century historical events.

12.1.11 Students will demonstrate historical research and geographical skills by:
- Identifying, analyzing, and interpreting primary and secondary sources and artifacts.
- Validating sources as to their authenticity, authority, credibility, and possible bias.
- Constructing various time lines of key events, periods, and personalities since the 10th century.

12.3 United States History

12.3.10 Students will analyze and explain the Great Depression, explaining factors, such as:
- Causes and effects of changes in business cycles.
- Weaknesses in key sectors of the economy in the late 1920s. United States government economic policies in the late 1920s.
- Causes and effects of the Stock Market Crash.
- The impact of the Depression on the American people.

12.3.17 Students will develop skills for historical analysis, such as the ability to:
- Analyze documents, records, and data, such as artifacts, diaries, letters, photographs, journals, newspapers, and historical accounts.
- Evaluate the authenticity, authority, and credibility of sources.
- Formulate historical questions and defend findings based on inquiry and interpretation.
- Develop perspectives of time and place, such as the construction of various time lines of events, periods, and personalities in American history.
- Communicate findings orally, in brief analytical essays, and in a comprehensive paper.

Information Power Information Literacy Standards and Indicators: 1.1, 1.2, 1.3, 1.4, 1.5, 2.1, 2.2, 2.3, 2.4, 3.1, 3.2, 3.3, 3.4, 5.1, 5.2, 5.3, 6.1, 6.2, 9.1, 9.2, 9.3, 9.4

Cooperative Teaching Plan:

Library Media Specialist Will:

- Collaborate with classroom teacher to outline the unit, select topics, review the Big6™ process research model, and determine objectives.
- Introduce information on the Big6™ process research model and search strategies to students.
- Provide bookmarks outlining information resources and the Big6™ process research model.
- Provide note taking strategies and graphic organizers.
- Guide students in composing their research questions.
- Highlight a wide variety of appropriate information resources.
- Assist students in finding appropriate literary selections for their newspapers.
- Model the Big6™ process for a specific topic.
- Assist students in using information resources and graphic organizers.
- Conference with teacher and individual students about student progress and focus on specific skills with students who need assistance.

Teacher Will:

- Explain the overall unit, providing objectives, timelines, and expectations.
- Discuss major events of the eras that students will focus on so they can select a specific topic within the era (e.g., focus on the Great Depression of the 1930s).
- Drawing from the diversity of the students, arrange for speakers to present information about specific eras to the class.
- Prepare a list of literary works and show visuals from a variety of eras.
- Present expectations for journal writing and respond to daily student journal entries.
- Assist students in composing research questions and in following the Big6™ process.
- Explain and model the composition of the newspaper required as the final product.
- Create the assessment criteria and assess the final projects.

Resources:

Print

A variety of print resources on American decades, including:

Almanacs on American Life series. New York: Facts on File, 1995-2000.
Bruccoli, Matthew. J. and Richard Layman, eds. *American Decades* series. Detroit: Gale, 1994.
A Cultural History of the United States series. San Diego: Lucent Books, Inc., 1999.
Fashions of a Decade series. New York: Facts on File, 1990.
Grun, Bernard. *Timetables of History*. New York: Touchstone Books, 1991.
Haskell, Barbara. *The American Century: Art & Culture 1900–1950*. New York: W.W. Norton & Co., 1999.
LIFE magazines, bound volumes 1940-1995.
Moss, Joyce, and George Wilson. *Profiles in American History* series. Detroit: Gale Research, Inc., 1995.
Our American Century series. Alexandria, Virginia: Time-Life Books, 1998.
Press, David P. *Multicultural Portrait of America's Music*. New York: Marshall Cavendish, 1994.

Electronic

Online Databases (requiring subscription):
    Grolier Online
    Wilson Web
    EBSCOhost Web
American Memory: Historical Collections for the National Digital Library. 18 July 2002.
    24 July 2002 <http://memory.loc.gov>.
History with the History Net. 24 July 2002 <http://www.TheHistoryNet.com>.
The Library of Congress. 24 July 2002 <http://www.loc.gov>.
Whitley, Peggy. "American Cultural History: The Twentieth Century." Kingwood College
    Library. December 1999. 24 July 2002
    <http://www.nhmccd.edu/contracts/lrc/kc/decades.html>.

Audio-Visual

The 20th Century: 1900's–1990's. 10 videocassettes. MPI Home Video, 2000.

Equipment

Internet-accessible computers
LCD projector
Overhead projector

Product or Culminating Activity: Students create a facsimile newspaper covering key information from the selected era. It must include a feature article as well as at least one news article in each of the following areas: politics and government, science and technology, art and music, religion, sports and adventure, dress and food, and literature and writers. Newspapers are displayed on tri-fold posterboards. Orally, students present an overview of their newspapers to the class. Newspaper storyboards are then displayed in the library media center. Students may also choose from a variety of optional projects to complete for needed credit (displays, artwork, biographies, book reviews) in addition to the newspaper.

Assessment Overview: The classroom teacher uses a 100-point grading criterion for the newspaper. The media specialist and classroom teacher jointly give daily participation grades. (Because students are allowed to choose a topic of interest, they are actively engaged in the activity. Use of the Big6™ process research model and a variety of graphic organizers also adds to the success of the project because students are focused and ready to begin researching.)

Figure 4.34 **An Era in Time**

The Research Path

DEFINE THE TASK
What is the assignment? What do I need in order to accomplish it?
What questions do I have? Is my topic too broad/narrow?

CHOOSE THE BEST RESOURCES FOR THE TASK
What can I use to find the information I need?
What resources are the best?

FIND RELEVANT INFORMATION WITHIN THE RESOURCES
What can I use within the resources?
How can I find the relevant information?

USE THE INFORMATION
What do I need to read, view, listen to, or experience?
Are there graphic organizers I can use while taking notes?

ORGANIZE THE INFORMATION
How can I put my information together? What is my final product?

EVALUATION
How well did I accomplish my goal?
Have I found enough information?
Is my final product what I want it to be?

Figure 4.35 **An Era in Time**

Need an Idea? Eras to Consider...

Cold War	McCarthy era – 1950s	Renaissance
Jazz Age	Harlem Renaissance	U.S. Colonial Period
Elizabethan Era	French Revolution	Roaring Twenties
Old West	Any war of your choice	Westward Expansion
Gold Rush	Rock and Roll	Beatlemania
Early Immigration of 1900s	Holocaust	1950s
1960s	Settlement of Lincoln, Nebraska	Great Depression
Asian Dynasties	Aztecs	Incas
Ancient Egypt	Ancient Greece	Early Christianity
Space Age/Exploration	Pompeii	

Questions to Consider...

When was this period and where did it take place?

Who were the people involved? Role models?

What were the major events of the era?

What was the effect of this era on life or society?

What were the developments in science, art, music, medicine, technology, culture, dress, food?

What unique events/things happened during this time?

Figure 4.36   **An Era in Time**

KWL Sheet

What I KNOW, what I WANT to know, what I have LEARNED

Topic: _____

Key words related to your topic (synonyms, variant spellings, proper names, plurals, etc.):

Resources I can use:

What I already know	Questions?	What I've learned	Source

Figure 4.37   **An Era in Time**

Organizational QUAD Sheet

(Questions, Answers, Details)

Topic: _____   Name: _____

QUESTIONS	ANSWERS	DETAILS
1.		
2.		
3.		
4.		
5.		

	REFERENCES	
AUTHOR	TITLE, COPYRIGHT	PAGE, VOLUME

Figure 4.38 **An Era in Time**

Double-Sided Bookmark

Library Media Center Information Sources

Card Catalog/Books—use a variety of keywords & subjects

Reference area—specialized books & encyclopedias, including collective biographies

Atlas—oversized books on atlas stand

Almanac

Dictionary

Vertical File

Biographies—**92** and **920**

Magazines & Newspapers

Community resources—people/places

Interviews

Videos & non-print materials

Electronic Databases

EBSCO—index of magazine and newspaper articles, health resources, animal encyclopedia, general encyclopedia, ERIC

SIRS—full text magazine & newspaper articles including government, arts & humanities

TOPIC SEARCH—full text articles from magazines, newspapers, biographies, book reviews, opinion polls, government, current events

GROLIER'S ENCYCLOPEDIAS

WILSON WEB—biographies with photos & full text business, science, social science, arts & humanities journal articles

Internet Sites

Library Spot

Internet Public Library—"Teen" & "Youth" categories

iNet Library—Go to School section, then to Subject Areas

Subject Areas icon—US/World history, career, science, medical, literature, Nebraska Web sites

Library Media Center Search Strategies

Pre-plan your search strategies!

Things to think about:
Choose your topic:

_____

_____

What do I want to know?

Is my topic too narrow/broad?

What do I think I already know?

What questions should I ask?

What is my central search question?

What are my keywords? (Synonyms, plurals, related terms, various spellings, proper names)

What might my completed project look like?

Who will be my audience?

Do I need to change my topic?

What resources are available?

| Figure 4.39 | An Era in Time |

Newspaper Grading Form

Name: _____   **Total Points:** _____

FRONT PAGE DESIGN (5 points each, 40 points total)   **Total** _____
Front page should include:
       A title for your newspaper
       8 appropriate headlines (for the articles)
       8 articles, including the feature article
       Date
       Edition
       Appropriate logo
       Pictures, photographs, or graphics
       Table of Contents

ARTICLES (20 points)   **Total** _____
Articles for each of these areas:
       Feature story
       Politics & Government
       Science & Technology
       Art & Music
       Religion
       Sports & Adventure
       Dress & Food
       Literature & Writers

OVERALL APPEARANCE (15 points)   **Total** _____
       Appropriate columns
       Spacing, proportion, & balance
       Appropriate font & size (12)

PARTICIPATION & COMMUNICATION (10 points)   **Total** _____
Areas to be evaluated:
       Communication between members of the group
       Equal distribution of the labor
       Time spent on task

CREATIVITY—10 points   **Total** _____

DEADLINE—5 points   **Total** _____

                                 PROJECT TOTAL POINTS _____

Comments:

"Extreme Themes" of World War II

Gail Barraco, Library Media Specialist
Barbara Case, Global History Teacher
Groton High School
400 Peru Road, Groton, New York 13073
607-898-5803
gbarraco@btboces.org

Grade Level: 10

Unit Overview: The devastation of World War II changed maps, took millions of lives, and wreaked vast physical and emotional damage across Europe, Asia, and the Pacific. The growing tensions among nations before and after World War II, as well as the hope for peaceful solutions to international disputes helped shape our world today. There were many perspectives and responses to specific events throughout World War II. In order to become familiar with these multiple perspectives, students complete one Document Analysis Sheet for each document they analyze, then write an essay pertaining to a document-based-question.

Time Frame: one week

Content Area Standards: New York State Learning Standards <http://www.nysatl.nysed.gov/standards.html>

Social Studies

Standard 2: World History Commencement Level Students will use a variety of intellectual skills to demonstrate their understanding of major ideas, era, themes, developments, and turning points in world history and examine the broad sweep of history from a variety of perspectives.

2.1 The study of world history requires an understanding of world cultures and civilizations, including an analysis of important ideas, social and cultural values, beliefs, and traditions. This study also examines the human condition and the connections and interactions of people across time and space and the ways different people view the same event or issue from a variety of perspectives. Students will:

- define culture and civilization, explaining how they developed and changed over time. Investigate the various components of cultures and civilizations including social customs, norms, values, and traditions; political systems; economic systems; religions and spiritual beliefs; and socialization or educational practices
- understand the development and connectedness of Western civilization and other civilizations and cultures in many areas of the world and over time
- analyze historic events from around the world by examining accounts written from different perspectives
- understand the broad patterns, relationships, and interactions of cultures and civilizations during particular eras and across eras
- analyze changing and competing interpretations of issues, events, and developments throughout world history.

Standard 3: Geography Commencement Level Students will use a variety of intellectual skills to demonstrate their understanding of the geography of the interdependent world in which we live—local, national, and global—including the distribution of people, places, and environments over the earth's surface.

3.1 Geography can be divided into six essential elements which can be used to analyze important historic, geographic, economic, and environmental questions and issues. These six elements include: the world in spatial terms, places and regions, physical settings (including natural resources), human systems, environment and society, and the use of geography. (Adapted from *The National Geography Standards, 1994: Geography for Life*). Students will:
- understand how to develop and use maps and other graphic representations to display geographic issues, problems, and questions
- describe the physical characteristics of the Earth's surface and investigate the continual reshaping of the surface by physical processes and human activities
- investigate the characteristics, distribution, and migration of human populations on the Earth's surface (Taken from *National Geography Standards, 1994*)
- understand the development and interactions of social/cultural, political, economic, and religious systems in different regions of the world
- analyze how the forces of cooperation and conflict among people influence the division and control of the Earth's surface (Taken from *National Geography Standards, 1994*)
- explain how technological change affects people, places, and regions.

Standard 4: Economics Commencement Level Students will use a variety of intellectual skills to demonstrate their understanding of how the United States and other societies develop economic systems and associated institutions to allocate scarce resources; how major decision-making units function in the United States and other national economies; and how an economy solves the scarcity problem through market and non-market mechanisms.

4.1 1. The study of economics requires an understanding of major economic concepts and systems, the principles of economic decision making, and the interdependence of economies and economic systems throughout the world. Students will:
- analyze the effectiveness of varying ways societies, nations, and regions of the world attempt to satisfy their basic needs and wants by utilizing scarce resources
- define and apply basic economic concepts such as scarcity, supply/demand, opportunity, costs, production, resources, money and banking, economic growth, markets, costs, competition, and world economic systems
- understand the nature of scarcity and how nations of the world make choices which involve economic and social costs and benefits
- describe the ideals, principles, structure, practices, accomplishments, and problems related to the United States economic system
- compare and contrast the United States economic system with other national economic systems, focusing on the three fundamental economic questions
- explain how economic decision making has become global as a result of an interdependent world economy
- understand the roles in the economic system of consumers, producers, workers, investors, and voters.

Information Power Information Literacy Standards and Indicators: 1.1, 1.2, 1.4, 1.5, 2.1, 2.2, 2.3, 2.4, 3.1, 3.2, 3.3, 3.4

Cooperative Teaching Plan:

Library Media Specialist Will:
- Instruct students in and reinforce the following skills:
  - Use of Internet Hotlist (see Resources) for links to Internet sites in Filamentality to locate resources on selected topic.
  - Location of additional materials in Dynix WebPac, the automated catalog.
  - The utility of print reference tools found in the library media center for primary source documents.
  - The process for using the Nueva Research site (see Resources) for citing references, both print and electronic.
  - Cutting and pasting citations formatted from the Nueva site into *Microsoft Word* for a "Works Cited" page.
- Answer student questions about correct citing.
- Provide access to materials not available in our library through interlibrary loan.
- Monitor student progress in locating materials, analyzing information, and applying this information in their essays.

Teacher Will:
- Instruct students on the requirements for the project.
- Review the DBQ Grid/analysis sheets which guide students in construction of the essay.
- Review the rubric which will be used to evaluate student performance on the essay.
- Offer examples of World War II events that constitute "Extreme Themes," e.g. Hitler's concept of Aryan racial domination; the Japanese invasion of Nanking; the Bataan Death March; Japanese Internment.
- Assist in and monitor student progress in locating, analyzing and applying information.
- Assess student essays.

Resources:

Print
Bigelow, Barbara C. *World War II: Primary Sources*. Boston, Massachusetts: UXL, 1999.

The New Grolier Encyclopedia of World War II. Danbury, Connecticut: Grolier Educational Corporation, 1995.

Parrish, Thomas. *The Simon and Schuster Encyclopedia of World War II*. New York: Simon and Schuster, 1978.

Peduzzi, Kelli. *America in the 20th Century: 1940-1949*. New York: Marshall Cavendish, 1995.

Twentieth Century America: A Primary Source Collection from the Associated Press. Danbury, Connecticut: Grolier Educational Corporation, 1995.

Electronic
Barraco, Gail and Barbara Case. *A Hotlist on World War II*. 22 March 2001. 24 July 2002 <http://www.kn.pacbell.com/wired/fil/pages/listworldwamr27.html>.

"Document Analysis Worksheets." *The National Archives and Records Administration*. 24 July 2002. 24 July 2002 <http://www.nara.gov/education/teaching/analysis/analysis.html>.

"Research." *Nueva Library Page.* 1 July 2002. 24 July 2002
<http://nuevaschool.org/~debbie/library/research/research.html>.

Product or Culminating Activity: Students analyze an array of documents—photographs, political cartoons, posters, maps, artifacts, sound recordings, motion pictures—then assess the point of view of the person who created the document and its relevance to the topic. Students identify the opinion being expressed and analyze the presentation of factual information, using critical thinking skills to integrate their knowledge of world history and their knowledge of the primary source documents. They write an essay that successfully depicts the "extreme themes" of World War II, addressing the accuracy of President Roosevelt's prediction that World War II would be a "War of Survival," and incorporating at least three of the World War II themes into their evaluation: politics; social life and culture; economics; key individuals; extremism; and science and technology.

Assessment Overview: The classroom teacher grades the essays based on a rubric modified for this topic from the New York State Global Studies Regents Exam.

Figure 4.40   *"Extreme Themes" of World War II*

Essay Guidelines and Themes

Using information from the documents and your knowledge of global history, address the following topics in a well-prepared and complete essay:

The accuracy of President Roosevelt's prediction that World War II would be a "War of Survival." Incorporate at least three of the World War II themes into your evaluation: politics; social life and culture; economics; key individuals; extremism; and science and technology.

For example:

EXTREMISM:
- Adolf Hitler's idea of Aryan racial domination not only brought about WWII in Europe but also led to the Holocaust.
- The Japanese invasion of Nanking in 1937 involved mass shootings and terrible brutality — 250,000 Chinese were killed. It has been referred to as the "Rape of China."
- In the Philippines, Japanese soldiers forced American and Filipino POW's to march while they beat, stabbed, and shot them in an event that became known as the Bataan Death March.
- In Poland, Soviet Troops forced thousands of Poles to endure imprisonment, torture, and execution.
- In the United States, Japanese-Americans were forced into internment camps.

ECONOMICS:
- Germany and Japan wanted to obtain the material resources that would enable them to be powerful industrial states.
- The United States became the arsenal of the Allied powers; it produced the military equipment the Allies needed for the war. This shaped the American economy.
- World War II became a global war, and women were expected to support the war cause in many European nations, as well as the United States.

SOCIAL LIFE AND CULTURE:
- Many people became homeless refugees from WWII.
- Many children were evacuated from the cities to escape bombings, but they also became orphans.
- In Eastern Europe, Germans closed and destroyed many schools.
- Propaganda was used extensively throughout the war.

KEY INDIVIDUALS:
- Adolf Hitler
- Joseph Stalin
- Franklin Delano Roosevelt
- Benito Mussolini
- Charles de Gaulle
- Winston Churchill

Figure 4.40 (continued from page 115)

SCIENCE AND TECHNOLOGY:

- New weapons of mass destruction
- Sonar to detect subs
- Improved planes
- Radar to detect planes
- Aircraft carriers
- Medical advancements to treat wounds
- New bombs
- Fast moving armored tanks
- Walkie talkies
- Machine guns

POLITICS:

- The war caused the destruction of governments, created political chaos, and led to the emergence of two, new superpowers—the United States and the Soviet Union.

| Figure 4.41 | "Extreme Themes" of World War II |

DBQ Grid

* Must use half + one of all documents given

Paragraph 1 Introduction:

Paragraph 2 Documents Used:

Paragraph 3 Documents Used:

Paragraph 4 Documents Used:

Outside Information on Topic:

Paragraph 5 Conclusion:

Reminders/checklist:
DID YOU: ___Re-read the essay question and your essay?   ___leave the reader a sense that points are tied together and summed up? ___check that no opinion is present in the conclusion?

Figure 4.42   *"Extreme Themes" of World War II*

DBQ Grid

*Must use half plus one of all documents given

Paragraph 1 Introduction:
1. Must be more than **3–4 sentences**.
2. Should reword the essay question/task, **do not copy** word for word.
3. Must include **time and place** (setting and approximate date, etc.).
4. Must have a **thesis statement**—takes the essay question and specifies what topics will be in the essay body paragraphs.

Paragraph 2 Documents Used:
1. Must begin each paragraph with a topic sentence.
2. **Cite documents** to support points by number or title/author.
3. Explain documents used in detail; any names or terms used must be defined and described.
4. Body paragraphs should be **lengthy**.
5. Must include references to a **time and place**.
6. **Check the task question, are you still on track?**

Paragraph 3 Documents Used:

Paragraph 4 Documents Used:

Outside Information on Topic:
Facts related to essay topic that are **not in the documents**
Once you have filled in this box, draw arrows from facts to body paragraphs they may be supporting details for. (Plan where you will use them.)

Paragraph 5 Conclusion:
1. Re-read the essay question and your essay.
2. Sum up the main idea of the essay—but DO NOT RECOPY YOUR INTRO!
3. Must be at least 2-3 sentences.
4. Should leave the reader with clear sense that all key points are summed up and tied together.
5. Do not use opinion in your conclusion.

Reminders/Checklist:
DID YOU: ___Re-read the essay question and your essay?   ___leave the reader a sense that points are tied together and summed up?   ___check that no opinion is present in the conclusion?

Figure 4.43 *"Extreme Themes" of World War II*

Rubric

5	■ addresses all aspects of tasks by analyzing and interpreting at least 3 themes/documents ■ thoroughly evaluates Roosevelt's prediction that World War II was a "war of survival" ■ incorporates information from documents and cites from the document but does not copy entire document ■ takes into account the point of view of the authors ■ essay is well-developed, consistently demonstrating a logical and clear plan of organization ■ introduces theme beyond simple restatement of task or historical context
4	■ addresses all aspects of tasks ■ limited evaluation of Roosevelt's prediction that WWII was a "war of survival" ■ incorporates information from documents but may cite incorrectly ■ incorporates relevant outside information ■ includes relevant facts, examples and details but discussion may be more descriptive than analytical ■ well-developed, logical and clear plan of organization ■ introduces theme beyond simple restatement of task
3	■ addresses most aspects of task in a limited way, using some of the documents ■ unequal treatment of tasks, one or part may be missing ■ incorporates limited or no relevant outside information ■ repeating task and historical context ■ includes some facts but discussion more descriptive than analytical ■ satisfactorily developed, general plan of organization
2	■ attempts to address some of task, limited use of documents ■ may evaluate only one theme ■ no relevant outside information ■ few facts, discussion restates contents of documents ■ poorly organized essay, lacking focus ■ fails to introduce or summarize theme
1	■ limited understanding of task with vague, unclear reference to documents ■ no relevant outside information ■ incorporates little or no accurate or relevant facts ■ attempts to complete task but major weaknesses in organization ■ fails to introduce or summarize theme
0	■ fails to address task, illegible, blank paper

Note: Rubric adapted from the Generic Scoring Rubric for the Document-Based Question of the New York State Regents' Examination
<http://www.emsc.nysed.gov/ciai/testing/socstre/gh&usinfo.html>

Literature Genre Study

Nicki Hansen, Library Media Specialist
Cindy Paul, Eighth Grade Language Arts Teacher
Kyrene Altadeña Middle School
14620 South Desert Foothills Parkway, Phoenix, Arizona 85048
480-783-1386
nhanse@kyrene.org

Grade Level: 8

Unit Overview: In Literature Genre Study, the Library Media Specialist and Language Arts Teacher collaborate to share literature appreciation and an in-depth study of historical fiction, science fiction, and fantastic fiction with eighth grade students. Following initial genre lessons every four to five weeks, students select a book from the genre. Lessons include an introduction to the elements of the genre, discussion of well-known authors and titles, critical thinking and/or author study activities, required projects, and assessment rubrics. The teacher and LMS collaborate on follow-up writing and related genre activities. Each genre study period culminates in a student-selected project as well as opportunities to display multimedia and critical thinking skills.

Time Frame: 16-20 weeks

Content Area Standards: The study unit incorporates both Kyrene School District Standards for Language Arts-8th grade and the Arizona State Content Standards-Language Arts.
<http://www.ade.state.az.us/standards/contentstandards.asp>

Standard 1-Reading (Grades 6-8)
- R-E2. Use reading strategies such as making inferences and predictions, summarizing, paraphrasing, differentiating fact from opinion, drawing conclusions, and determining the author's purpose and perspective to comprehend written selections
  PO 1. Identify the main ideas; critical and supporting details; and the author's purpose, feelings and point of view of the text
  PO 2. Distinguish fact from opinion
  PO 3. Summarize the text in own words (assessed at district level only)
  PO 4. Compare and contrast the text (e.g., characters, genre, cultural differences, fact, fiction)
  PO 5. Determine cause-and-effect relationships
  PO 6. Summarize the text in chronological, sequential or logical order
  PO 7. Predict outcome of text
- R-E3. Analyze selections of fiction, nonfiction and poetry by identifying the plot line (i.e., beginning, conflict, rising action, climax and resolution); distinguishing the main character from minor ones; describing the relationships between and motivations of characters; and making inferences about the events, setting, style, tone, mood and meaning of the selection
  PO 1. Describe the setting and its relationship to the selection
  PO 2. Describe the motivation of major and minor characters in a selection
  PO 3. Draw defensible conclusions, based on stated and implied information according to style, meaning and mood

PO 4. Differentiate fiction, nonfiction or poetry based on their attributes

PO 5. Identify the theme

- R-E4. Identify the author's purpose, position, bias and strategies in a persuasive selection

PO 1. Identify the author's purpose and use of details to support the purpose

PO 3. Identify the author's bias

Standard 2-Writing (Grades 6-8)

- W-E2. Write a personal experience narrative or creative story that includes a plot and shows the reader what happens through well-developed characters, setting, dialog, and themes and uses figurative language, descriptive words and phrases

PO 2. Write a story

- develop a story line in a sequence that is clear
- develop the characters
- describe the setting
- use dialog when appropriate
- use simile, metaphor or descriptive words and phrases

- W-E3. Write a summary that presents information clearly and accurately, contains the most significant details and preserves the position of the author

PO 1. Use own words except for material quoted

PO 2. Preserve the author's perspective and voice

PO 3. Contain main ideas of event/article/story plus the most significant details

PO 4. Present clearly written and organized information

- W-E4. Write an expository essay that contains effective introductory and summary statements and fully develops the ideas with details, facts, examples and descriptions

PO 1. Write an expository essay that begins by stating the thesis (purpose) with an effective introductory statement or paragraph; provides smooth transitions; and ends with either a paragraph concluding the development of the thesis, a summary or a clincher statement

PO 2. Use own words (except for quoted material) to develop ideas accurately and clearly with supporting details, facts, examples or descriptions

PO 3. Use personal interpretation, analysis, evaluation or reflection to evidence understanding of subject

- W-E5. Write a report that conveys a point of view and develops a topic with appropriate facts, details, examples and descriptions from a variety of cited sources

PO 1. Write a report in own words (except for material quoted) that states, develops and provides a concluding statement for a point of view (perspective) about a topic that is narrow enough to be adequately covered

PO 2. Organize a report with a clear beginning, middle and end including use of smooth transitions

PO 3. Provide support through facts, details, examples or descriptions that are appropriate, directly related to the topic, and from a variety of cited sources

PO 4. Use personal interpretation, analysis, evaluation or reflection to evidence understanding of subject

- W-E7. Write a response to a literary selection by supporting their ideas with references to the text, other works or experiences

PO 1. State clearly a position that is interpretive, analytic, evaluative, or reflective

PO 2. Support references and conclusions with examples from the text, personal experience, references to other works or reference to non-print media

PO 3. Relate own ideas to supporting details in a clear and logical manner

PO 4. Provide support adequate to the literary selection (e.g., short poem vs. novel)

- W-E8. Demonstrate research skills using reference materials such as a dictionary, encyclopedia and thesaurus to complete effectively a variety of writing tasks

  PO 1. Implement a research strategy that includes
  - selecting best source for specific research purpose
  - taking notes that summarize and paraphrase information relevant to the topic
  - incorporating notes into a finished product

Standard 3-Listening and Speaking (Grades 6-8)
ESSENTIALS (Grades 4-8)

- LS-E2. Prepare and deliver an oral report in a content area and effectively convey the message through verbal and nonverbal communications with a specific audience

AZ Standard 4-Viewing and Presenting (Grades 6-8)
ESSENTIALS (Grades 4-8)

- VP-E2. Plan, develop and produce a visual presentation, using a variety of media such as videos, films, newspapers, magazines and computer images

Information Power Information Literacy Standards and Indicators: 1.1, 1.2, 1.3, 1.4, 1.5, 2.1, 2.2, 2.3, 2.4, 3.1, 3.2, 3.3, 3.4, 4.2, 5.1, 5.2, 5.3, 6.1, 6.2, 7.1, 7.2, 8.1, 8.2, 8.3, 9.1, 9.2, 9.3, 9.4

Cooperative Teaching Plan:

Library Media Specialist Will:
- Collaborate to prepare unit, activities, assessment rubrics, and to meet specific outcomes.
- Introduce each genre lesson and activities: historical fiction, fantastic fiction, and science fiction approximately 4-6 weeks apart.
- Introduce elements of each genre, critical thinking, and author study activities.
- Prepare overheads for use during introduction to historical fiction and fantastic fiction.
- Prepare *PowerPoint* presentation for use during introduction to science fiction.
- Select demonstration fiction and reference books, short stories, picture books prior to each genre introduction.
- Contact and schedule the speakers, schedule room use, publish schedule, and set-up.
- Select and purchase a wide selection of genre-specific fiction books for the library.
- Select and purchase a wide selection of reference books and materials.
- Interloan genre-specific books from other schools.
- Assist students in selection of an appropriate book for each featured genre.
- Collaborate on follow-up activities and incorporate writing and related genre activities.
- Suggest print and Internet resources during student research in the library.
- Assist teacher in computer lab as students prepare multimedia presentations.
- Assist teacher in assessing genre-related presentations and written assignments.

Teacher Will:
- Collaborate to prepare unit, activities, assessment rubrics and to meet specific outcomes.
- Collaborate to make arrangements for speakers during the science fiction study period.
- Teach students to write based on the Six Trait Writing Rubric.
- Teach students to write a persuasive essay.
- Assign students to gather information on an historical element from an historical fiction book.
- Incorporate follow-up activities and writing and related genre activities during the time students are reading on their own.

- Work with library media specialist to ensure each student has selected an appropriate (genre-specific, grade level and reading level appropriate) book of the featured genre.
- Assess presentations and written assignments for each grading period.

Resources:

Print

Adamson, Lynda G. *Recreating the Past: A Guide to American and World Historical Fiction For Children and Young Adults.* Westport, Connecticut: Greenwood Press, 1994.

Baldick, Chris. *The Concise Oxford Dictionary of Literary Terms.* New York: Oxford University Press, 1990.

But That's Another Story: Famous Authors Introduce Popular Genres. New York: Walker, 1996.

Card, Orson Scott. *How to Write Science Fiction and Fantasy.* Cincinnati, Ohio: Writer's Digest Books, 1990.

Clute, John. *Science Fiction: The Illustrated Encyclopedia.* New York: Dorling Kindersley, 1995.

The Concise Oxford Dictionary of Literary Terms. New York: Oxford Press, 1990.

Encyclopedia Americana. Danbury, Connecticut: Grolier, 2001.

Hartman, Donald K and Gregg Sapp. *Historical Figures in Fiction.* Phoenix: Oryx Press, 1994.

Herald, Diana Tixier. *Genreflecting: A Guide To Reading Interests in Genre Fiction.* Englewood, Colorado: Libraries Limited, 1995.

Morris, Patricia S. *Science Fiction and Fantasy.* West Nyack, New York: Center for Applied Research in Education, 1992.

New Book of Knowledge. Danbury, Connecticut: Grolier 2001.

Rovin, Jeff. *Aliens, Robots, and Spaceships.* New York: Facts on File, 1995.

Science Fiction, Fantasy, and Horror Writers: Volume 1, A-J. New York: UXL, 1995.

Science Fiction, Fantasy, and Horror Writers: Volume 2, K-Z. New York: UXL, 1995.

Teeters, Peggy. *Jules Verne: The Man Who Invented Tomorrow.* New York: Walker, 1992.

Van Vliet, Lucille W. *Approaches to Literature Through Genre.* Phoenix: Oryx Press, 1992.

World Book Encyclopedia. Chicago: World Book, Inc., 2001.

A large selection of classic and contemporary YA fiction novels to display, booktalk, and have available for checkout, by authors who are well known for writing in a specific genre. (Local and visiting authors spark the most interest.) Some examples include:

HISTORICAL FICTION: James Fenimore Cooper, Kathryn Lasky, Carolyn Meyer, Scott O'Dell, Ann Rinaldi, Theodore Taylor, H.H. Vick, and Lawrence Yep.

SCIENCE FICTION: Ray Bradbury, John Christopher, Arthur C. Clarke, Robert A. Heinlein, H.G. Wells, and Jules Verne.

FANTASTIC FICTION: T.A. Barron, Frank L. Baum, Lewis Carroll, Brian Jacques, Tamora Pierce, Robin McKinley, Philip Pullman, and J.R.R. Tolkien.

A selection of picture books to introduce the elements of historical fiction and fantastic fiction.

Periodicals in which science/technological innovation is regularly reported to demonstrate how themes in Science Fiction novels change as technology and science change. Examples, which may be most familiar to YA readers, include: *National Geographic, Newsweek, Popular Mechanics, Popular Science, Time,* and *U.S. World and News Report.*

Electronic

"Assessment: 6+1™ Trait Writing." *Northwest Regional Educational Laboratory*. 24 July 2002
  < http://www.nwrel.org/assessment/department.asp?d=1>.
Best Search Engines, Internet Directories, and Specialized Search Engines. 14 Jan. 2002
  <http://startingpage.com/html/search.html>.
Central Intelligence Agency Publications and Reports. 8 July 2002. 24 July 2002
  <http://www.cia.gov/cia/publications/pubs.html>.
Facts on File World News Digest 1980–2002. 2001
  <http://www.2facts.com/stories/mainmenu.asp>. (Requires subscription.)
Infoplease.com: Biography. 24 July 2002 <http://infoplease.lycos.com/people.html?iphp>.
The Library of Congress. 24 July 2002 <http://www.loc.gov/>.
National Geographic Online (maps, photography, travel, more). 24 July 2002
  <http://www.nationalgeographic.com/>.
Pirates! Fact & Legend. 24 July 2002 <http://www.piratesinfo.com/main.php>.
"6+1™ Writing: Assessment Scoring Guide." *Northwest Regional Educational Laboratory*.
  24 July 2002 <http://www.nwrel.org/assessment/pdfRubrics/6plus1traits.pdf>.
Smithsonian Institution. 24 July 2002 <http://www.si.edu/portal/t1-research.htm>.
States and Capitals. 24 July 2002 <http://www.50states.com/>.
World Book Online. 24 July 2002 <http://www.worldbookonline.com/>. (Requires subscription)
The World War I Document Archive. July 2002. 24 July 2002 <http://www.lib.byu.edu/~rdh/wwi/>.

Equipment

Computer projection system and laptop or computer workstation, overhead projector, projector screen.

Human

Local community speakers with a knowledge of or interest in the possibility of life forms beyond Earth, including a university astronomy professor; an NBC-affiliate reporter who is most often assigned to local UFO sightings; and a leader in the local Mutual UFO Network (MUFON).

Product or Culminating Activity: After reading a historical fiction book, students identify the 10 elements/clues of historical fiction in the book, then choose one time-period element to research. They present their research in a five-minute informational speech to the class.

While reading science fiction, students listen to a variety of speakers and write a persuasive essay about the possibility of life beyond earth. Students also recreate an accurate depiction of technology from a science fiction novel and orally explain the impact this technology had on the story resolution.

Working in groups of two to three and using media of their choice, (video with audio, *PowerPoint, HyperStudio,* or a Web site) students create a media invitation to a celebration that would appeal to the main characters in the fantasy book the group has read.

In a final, all-encompassing spring project, students demonstrate their creativity and writing skills as they write a short book, incorporating the elements of the genre with which they are most interested.

Assessment Overview: The library media specialist and the teacher jointly assess each culminating activity using rubrics.

Figure 4.44   **Literature Genre Study**

Historical Fiction 10 Clues

Choose a book from the historical fiction literature genre to read and then apply 10 clues of historical fiction to your book. For each clue, identify at least one element that you found in your book. You will also need to tell why each clue was significant in your book and its time period. As you know, every book of this genre may not address all clues. If one of these clues does not appear in your book, write NOT APPLICABLE. (You should be able to apply at least eight out of 10 clues to your historical fiction book).

1. A famous person and why this person is significant to this time period.

2. Groups of people significant to the story and why.

3. Names of special places significant to the story and why.

4. Geographical areas (rivers, mountain ranges, canals, etc.) and why these are significant in this time period.

5. Food and why this food is mentioned as particularly significant to the time period of your book.

6. Clothing and how it is indicative of this time period.

7. Items of special importance to the period of time (household or work items) and why.

8. Colorful or special language (an unfamiliar way of speaking) and why this is indicative of the time period.

9. Events and how these are significant to and/or indicative of the time period.

10. Transportation and why this is an example of a mode of transportation for this time period.

Figure 4.45   **Literature Genre Study**

That Was Then, This Is Now

Choose a historical fiction book about a time period that you find intriguing. (The library media specialist can help you find an appropriate book.) After reading the book and identifying the 10 clues for identifying a work of historical fiction, choose one of the historical elements to research. Use at least five different sources (Honors classes will use a minimum of eight), synthesize your information, and prepare a five-minute informational speech to present to the class. As part of your presentation, you must read aloud the passage in your book that makes reference to the aspect of history about which you are presenting. Turn in a Works Cited page, appropriately formatted. You will be assessed on your overall presentation using the following checklist.

Speech Skills Checklist

☐ Student summarizes the historical fiction book they read in no more than five spoken sentences.

☐ Student reads passage aloud from book to introduce the historical subject to the audience.

☐ Student has appropriate number of resources and completes a Works Cited page, appropriately formatted.

☐ The information is accurately and clearly presented.

☐ The student speaks for the appropriate amount of time.
(No longer than five minutes, and no fewer than four)

☐ Eye contact is made with audience members throughout room. Notes are referred to occasionally, not constantly.

☐ Voice level is loud enough to be easily heard by all audience members. Voice variation (tone) is demonstrated—not monotone.

☐ Body language and posture is strong and confident. Student stands tall and straight, using appropriate hand gestures, with no shifting or swaying.

☐ Visuals and props are present and used to help present information and maintain audience interest.

☐ Appropriate dress and pleasant manner is displayed.

_____ **Total Score**

Figure 4.46   **Literature Genre Study**

Science Fiction Author Motivation

Working in groups at your table, review the packet of author information about one of the SF authors to whom you were introduced today. Your group will quickly divide up the resources and skim for information to find answers to the following. Complete sentences are not necessary.

1. SF Author _____/Nationality_____

2. Life span _____ (yrs.)

3. Wrote from _____ to _____ (yrs.)

4. *Significant* technology (and dates of each) developed during this author's life (that may have influenced the author's writings):
   - ■
   - ■
   - ■

5. WHO influenced this author to write SF: Family/Friends/other authors
   WHAT influenced this author to write SF (list each that apply):
   - ■ Favorite books/authors
   - ■ Education
   - ■ Interests
   - ■ Other

6. What impact did this author have on the genre of science fiction? (Why is he/she well known for science fiction?)

7. List three of this author's best known SF titles/date of publication:
   1.
   2.
   3.

8. (OPTIONAL) 20th century scientists/authors/scientists who were influenced by this author's writing:

9. (OPTIONAL) What technology did this author "foresee" and include in his/her stories:

Figure 4.47   Literature Genre Study

Persuasive Essay on Scientific Theory

You will have an opportunity to hear a series of speakers including an astronomer, a news reporter, and a UFO proponent, each speaking on the possibility of life beyond Earth. You will take notes during each presentation. At the conclusion of all three presentations, you will take a position based on the presentations.

You will write a persuasive essay in which you draw logical conclusions supported by examples drawn from the speakers' presentations. Your essay should follow the format of a standard five (5)-paragraph essay with a clear topic sentence that includes three (3) prongs. The persuasive position should be supported in the body of the essay with specific quotes and examples from the presentations. The essay will be graded using the Six Trait Writing Rubric. (You may want to have your work peer-edited before you submit this for a grade.)

40 POSSIBLE POINTS

40.   **An H.G. Wells Essay** takes a definitive persuasive stance on the possibility of life beyond Earth. Student follows the standard five-paragraph essay format. The clear topic sentence includes three prongs. These ideas are supported in the body of the essay with specific quotes and examples from the presentations. A concluding paragraph leaves the reader feeling convinced/persuaded.

30.   **A Jules Verne Essay** identifies a position on the possibility of life beyond Earth. Student follows the standard five-paragraph essay format. The topic sentence includes three prongs. These ideas are supported in the body of the essay with specific quotes and examples from the presentations. A concluding paragraph leaves the reader feeling somewhat convinced/persuaded.

20.   **A Flash Gordon Essay** identifies a position on the possibility of life beyond Earth. Student may have omitted one paragraph of a standard five-paragraph essay format. The topic sentence includes at least two prongs. The student may have difficulty with the organization of the five-paragraph format. Support may be vague or missing and not drawn from presentations. The concluding paragraph may be weak, leaving the reader unconvinced.

10.   **A Marvin the Martian Essay** makes a vague attempt to take a position on the possibility of life beyond Earth. Student does not follow the standard five-paragraph essay format. Topic sentence may be missing. Any supports, such as quotes or speaker examples, are weak or missing. After reading this essay the reader is unconvinced.

| Figure 4.48 | Literature Genre Study |

Techno Wizard

Science or technology are important factors in a science fiction story and usually have an impact on problem resolution. After reading a science fiction book, you will recreate an example of technology that was an integral part of the story and explain the impact this technology had on the story outcome. The recreation must be an accurate, original, three-dimensional depiction of the technology described in the book. Your recreation should replicate the author's description as closely as possible. Label your recreation with your name, the title of the book, and the author, for display in the library.

In addition, you will make an oral presentation to the class in which you briefly summarize your science fiction book (without giving away the ending) and then explain how the technology you have recreated (your book may have several from which to choose), was used to impact the story resolution. You must read the author's description of this technology to the class. Both your teacher and the library media specialist will assess your creation as follows:

Physical Description	10 Points (Techno-Wizard)	5 Points	0 Points
Structure	Technology recreation is three-dimensional.	Technology recreation is two-dimensional.	Technology recreation is absent.
Originality And Creativity	Technology recreation is designed and constructed by the student.	Technology recreation is commercially prepared.	Technology recreation is absent.
Accuracy	Technology recreation closely matches physical description in the book and student is able to convince the audience of accuracy by reading the applicable passage descriptions. Book is present and student reads the passage aloud.	Technology recreation some-what matches the technology described in the book and student is somewhat able to convince the audience.	Technology recreation does not match technology described in the book. Book is not present and passage is not read.
Oral Presentation	20 Points (Techno-Wizard)	10 Points	0 Points
Oral Interpretaion	Student clearly describes how the technology in the book impacted the story outcome. Examples and details are given to convince the audience of this impact.	Student is some-what able to convince the audience that the technology had an impact on the outcome of the story.	Student is unable to convince the audience of the impact the technology had on the outcome of the story.

Figure 4.49 Literature Genre Study

Fantasy Fiesta

Working in groups of two to three, choose and read a fantasy book that is age and reading level appropriate for each member of the group. If you are in doubt, check with your teacher or library media specialist. Then, using media of your choice (video with audio, *PowerPoint, HyperStudio*, or an Internet Web site), create a media invitation to a celebration that would appeal to the main characters in your book. As part of sharing your media presentation with the class, your group will give an oral summary of your book to help the audience understand the content of the invitation. Do not give away the ending. Book summaries should include a review of the elements of fantastic fiction discussed in class with regard to time, setting, plot, characters, and problem solving.

By reviewing the following information, you can determine your grade for this assignment. Review the attached "Tips for Success" before you begin and again before you finalize your presentation. It is expected that each person in the group will contribute equally.

5 **Spielberg Quality Presentation** includes the information of the five W's (who, what, when, where, and why) of the invitation. The media presentation thoroughly reflects an understanding of the media type chosen. The media presentation has been edited for audio, video, and text, and the resulting product looks professional. *PowerPoint* or *HyperStudio* presentations have at least 7 slides/cards. Videos are at least 3 minutes long and include a running title. A home page consists of one page with at least 6 hyperlinks.

4 **Lucas Quality Presentation** may not clearly state all five W's. The media presentation largely reflects an understanding of the media type chosen. The media presentation shows evidence of editing; however there may be an occasional flaw in audio, video, or text. *PowerPoint* or *HyperStudio* presentations have at least 6 slides/cards. Videos are at least 2.5 minutes long and include a running title. A home page consists of one page with 4 hyperlinks.

3 **Acme Quality Presentation** may not include the five W's. The media presentation reflects only some understanding of the media type chosen. The media presentation shows some evidence of editing, but there may be some flaws in audio, video, or text. *PowerPoint* or *HyperStudio* presentations have at least 5 slides/cards. Videos are at least 2 minutes long and include a running title. A home page consists of one page with only 2 hyperlinks.

2 **Apprentice Quality Presentation** omits most of the five W's. The media presentation does not reflect an understanding of the media type chosen. The media presentation lacks evidence of editing, and there are many flaws in audio, video, or text. *PowerPoint* or *HyperStudio* presentations appear incomplete with fewer than 5 slides/cards. Videos are short, less than 2 minutes long, and appear incomplete. A home page is incomplete.

0 **Smurf Quality Presentation.** The student/group failed to produce a presentation.

Figure 4.50 | **Literature Genre Study**

Fantasy Fiesta Tips For Success

1. The book you choose to read must be age and reading level appropriate for each member of your group. If you are in doubt, check with your teacher or library media specialist. Each person in your group must agree to read the same fantasy book.

2. Be kind to your audience who will be reading the slides/cards:
   - Use no more than 7 lines per slide/card. 3-4 lines are even better.
   - Use no more than 7 words per line. Fewer are easier to read at a distance.
   - Use colors for background, text, and graphics that are pleasing and easy to distinguish. Your audience should not have to struggle to discern the information you present.
   - Your book summary should be oral, not included in the required number of slides, cards, or minutes.
   - Do not use the "timer" if you are preparing a *PowerPoint* presentation. You should move the slides forward at your pace during the presentation.

3. You will be allowed only one spelling mistake. After that, one point will be deducted for each spelling error (use the spell check AND have someone from another team proof read your presentation before you finalize your work).

4. All of your "invitation" language must be in keeping with the book:
   - Use appropriate character communication: Don't say, "Please call 995-5000," if telephones were not mentioned in your book. Think! Would your characters use special language or method to communicate?
   - The party food should also be consistent with the diet of your characters (not pizza, if that is not in keeping with what the characters would normally eat).
   - The party location (setting) and time setting should also be consistent with the book. What is a logical place for the characters to meet for a celebration, and how is the concept of time best communicated? Be creative!
   - Any predicted events as part of the celebration should follow the story line, not create a new story line or be silly.

5. Each member of your group should save a current copy as your computer work progresses so that your work can be accessed even if one person is absent. Remember that projects with many graphics take up a lot of space, and you may be unable to save to a disk. Save to your personal network drive on the school server whenever possible. Also, if you choose to work at home, and your project is too large to save on a floppy disk, you may e-mail your project as an attachment to your teacher or library media specialist. If you work on a home computer, save your *PowerPoint* or *HyperStudio* presentation to the software version you will use at school during the time of the class presentation—the version currently installed at school. (Ignoring this tip may mean that you cannot access/pull-up your presentation on a school computer).
   - The school currently has the following software versions installed on all computers:
     PowerPoint version _____ (Record version here) and
     Hyper Studio version _____ (Record version here)
   - Save your completed computer work to the file folder named _____ under the _____ network drive for easy access during time of class presentations.
     (Students should record the computer *file folder* and *drive* specified by teacher and library media specialist)

The Long and the Short of It: The American Short Story

Diana G. Murphy, Head Library Media Specialist

Brad Kwiatek, Head of English Department

The Kiski School

1888 Brett Lane, Saltsburg, Pennsylvania 15681

724-639-3586

diana.murphy@kiski.org

Grade Level: 11 or 12

Unit Overview: The Long and the Short of It is a collaborative project between the library media center and Junior English teachers whose objective is to encourage students to become acquainted with many different short story authors and styles in a short time frame. Students work in groups, as well as individually, to learn writing skills, analysis of short story elements, and research skills. They also learn the use of the *Short Story Index*, short story anthologies, and biographical reference materials, as well as specific online short story and author resources. The culminating activity is a group discussion of card summaries of stories and a writing conference with the teacher and library media specialist.

Time Frame: Two weeks

Content Area Standards: Pennsylvania Academic Standards for Reading, Writing, Speaking and Listening
<http://www.bhasd.k12.pa.us/centraladmin/c&i/AcadStds%20Chapter%204/reading.pdf>

1.1 Learning to Read Independently.
1.1.11.A Locate various texts, media and traditional resources for assigned projects.
1.1.11.C Use knowledge of root words and words from literary works to recognize and understand the meaning of new words during reading.
1.1.11.G Demonstrate after reading understanding and interpretation of fiction text.

1.2 Reading Critically in All Content Areas
1.2.11.A. Read and understand essential content of text

1.3 Reading, Analyzing and Interpreting Literature
1.3.11.A Read and understand works of literature.
1.3.11.B Analyze the relationships, uses and effectiveness of literary elements used by one or more authors in similar genres including characterization, setting, plot, theme, point of view, tone and style.
1.3.11.C Analyze the effectiveness, in terms of literary quality of the author's use of literary devices.

1.4 Types of Writing
1.4.11.B Write complex informational pieces.
1.4.11.C Write persuasive pieces (clearly stated position or opinion with properly cited evidence).

1.5 Quality of Writing

1.5.11.A Write with a sharp, distinct focus.

1.5.11.B Write using well-developed content appropriate for the topic.

1.5.11.C Write with controlled and/or subtle organization.

1.5.11.D Write with a command of the stylistic aspects of composition.

1.8 Research

1.8.11.A Select and refine a topic for research.

1.8.11.B Locate information using appropriate sources and strategies.

1.8.11.C Organize, summarize and present the main ideas from research.

Information Power Information Literacy Standards and Indicators: 1.1, 1.2, 1.3, 1.4, 1.5, 2.1, 2.2, 2.4, 3.1, 3.2, 3.3, 3.4, 5.1, 5.2, 6.1, 6.2

Cooperative Teaching Plan:

Library Media Specialist Will:

- Introduce the unit, outlining objectives and requirements (with classroom teacher).
- Present information about short story authors from a collaboratively developed list, emphasizing type of stories with brief, interesting facts about authors and styles.
- Teach use of biographical references, and *Short Story Index.*
- Teach use of the database of authors, short stories, and sources (hard copy and online).
- Assist students in selection of author(s) and short stories (with classroom teacher).
- Assist students in location and evaluation of appropriate information on authors and location of chosen short stories (with classroom teacher).

Teacher Will:

- Introduce the unit, outlining objectives and requirements (with library media specialist).
- Use a classic short story, such as "Paul's Case" by Willa Cather, as an in-class reading and discussion tool to teach short story elements. Show portions of "Paul's Case" video.
- Answer student questions about their chosen authors and short stories.
- Assign reading of short stories as homework.
- Prepare students to write and share their completed card summaries in small groups and with teacher and library media specialist in a writing conference.
- Collect completed card summaries and assess achievement.

Resources:

Print

Boynton, Robert W. *Introduction to the Short Story.* Portsmouth, NJ: Boynton/Cook Publishers, 1985.

Fuller, Muriel. *More Junior Authors.* New York: H. W. Wilson Co, 1963.

Hooper, Brad. *The Short Story Readers' Advisory: A Guide to the Best.* Chicago: American Library Association, 2000.

Hooper, Brad. *Short Story Writers and Their Work: A Guide to the Best.* 2nd ed. Chicago: American Library Association, 1992.

Knight, Damon Francis. *Creating Short Fiction.* 1st ed. Cincinnati, Ohio: Writer's Digest Books, 1981.

Kunitz, Stanley J. and Howard Haycraft, eds. *American Authors, 1600-1900: A Biographical Dictionary of American Literature. Complete in one Volume with 1,300 Biographies and 400 Portraits.* New York: Wilson, 1938.

Kunitz, Stanley and Howard Haycraft. *The Junior Book of Authors.* 2d ed., rev. New York: Wilson, 1951.

Kunitz, Stanley and Howard Haycraft. *Twentieth Century Authors.* New York: Wilson, 1955.

Kunitz, Stanley and Vineta Colby. *European Authors, 1000–1900: A Biographical Dictionary of European Literature.* New York: Wilson, 1967.

Magill, Frank N., ed. *American Literature, Realism To 1945.* Pasadena, California: Salem Press, 1981.

Magill, Frank N., ed. *Cyclopedia of World Authors.* Englewood Cliffs, New Jersey: Salem Press, 1974.

Magill, Frank, N., ed. *Cyclopedia of Literary Characters.* Englewood Cliffs, New Jersey: Salem Press, 1963.

Magill, Frank N., ed. *Magill's Survey of American Literature.* New York: Marshall Cavendish: Salem Press, 1991.

Magill, Frank N., ed. *Masterpieces of African-American Literature.* 1st ed. New York: HarperCollins, 1992.

Magill, Frank N., ed. *Masterplots: 1,801 Plot Stories and Critical Evaluations of the World's Finest Literature.* Revised Second Edition. Pasadena, California: Salem Press, 1996.

Robinson, Lillian S., ed. and comp. *Modern Women Writers.* New York: Frederick Ungar: Continuum, 1996.

Ross, Danforth. *The American Short Story.* Minneapolis: University of Minnesota Press, 1961.

Short Story Index. New York: Wilson, 1950.

Unger, Leonard, ed. *American Writers: A Collection of Literary Biographies.* New York: Scribner, 1961.

Weaver, Gordon. *The American Short Story, 1945–1980: A Critical History.* Boston: Twayne, 1983.

Electronic

"Bibliomania: Short Stories." *Bibliomania.* 24 July 2002
<http://www.bibliomania.com/0/5/frameset.html>.

Classic Horror Short Stories: the Collection. 24 July 2002 <http://atoledo.freeyellow.com/>.

East of the Web-Short Stories. 24 July 2002 <http://www.short-stories.co.uk/>.

"Short Stories." *Classic Reader.* 24 July 2002 <http://classicreader.com/toc.php/sid.6/>.

The Short Story Classico: The Best from the Masters of the Genre. 24 July 2002
<http://www.geocities.com/short_stories_page/>.

Story Finder. Roth Publishing, (requires subscription) <http://www.rothpoem.com/index.html>.

Product or Culminating Activity: Group discussion of card summaries of stories and writing conference with teacher and library media specialist. Card summaries are evaluated by classroom teacher.

Assessment Overview: Library media specialist will evaluate student success based on observation of selection and use of sources and demonstration of mastery of information skills targeted. Mastery of Information Skills will be recorded in a database with student name and skills learned. Classroom teacher will evaluate card summaries, group participation, and writing skills using the Student Evaluation Rubric.

Figure 4.51   **The Long and the Short of It: The American Short Story**

American Short Story Authors

AIKEN, CONRAD . . . . .Writings show New England background and usually express the quest to find oneself.

ANDERSON, SHERWOOD . . . . . . .Stories of small-town people with a philosophy of life based on the primal forces of human behavior.

ASIMOV, ISAAC . . . . .Science fiction, best known for his Foundation Series.

BALDWIN, JAMES . . . . .Moved to Europe to escape racial prejudice, most writings deal with African American life in U.S.

BELLOW, SAUL . . . . .Born in Canada of Russian parents, he writes primarily about Jewish life in the U.S. and during the Holocaust.

BENCHLEY, ROBERT (father) and
BENCHLEY, NATHANIEL (son) . . . . .Humorists.

BENET, STEPHEN VINCENT . . . . . .Began writing in college about the American scene.

BIERCE, AMBROSE . . . . .Wrote tales of horror with surprise endings and realistic emotions.

BOYLE, KAY . . . . .Lived as an expatriate in France. Wrote of romance and WWII.

BRADBURY, RAY . . . . .Best known for macabre and humorous science fiction stories.

CANFIELD (FISHER), DOROTHY . . . .Writes about average people with average problems.

CAPOTE, TRUMAN . . . . .Stories about struggle against social restraint.

CATHER, WILLA . . . . .Early life in Nebraska among immigrant pioneers greatly influenced her writing.

CHEEVER, JOHN . . . . .Expulsion from a private school led to his literary career. Stories are usually humorous satirical studies of affluent New England families.

ELLISON, RALPH . . . . .Writes about young black men and their struggles with race and society.

FAULKNER, WILLIAM . . . . .Stories deal with a variety of topics but many are about the Old South and many are about military service in WWI.

FITZGERALD, F. SCOTT . . . . .Used the Jazz Age and the Roaring Twenties as the backdrop for most of his stories.

HEMINGWAY, ERNEST . . . . .Although best known for his novels, his stories also express "The Lost Generation" of society.

JACKSON, SHIRLEY . . . . .Disturbed adolescents provide the theme for most of her stories.

KING, STEPHEN . . . . .Stories, like his novels, are horror mysteries with underlying human frailty.

LARDNER, RING . . . . .Humorous satirical stories from a sportswriter's perspective.

Figure 4.51   **(continued from page 139)**

MALAMUD, BERNARD . . . . .Witty and satirical writer who uses sports and Jewish New York as his medium.

McCULLERS, CARSON . . . . .Searching for discovery of self, her stories are set in rural Georgia.

OATES, JOYCE CAROL . . . . .Savage psychological portrayals of demonic people.

O'CONNOR, FLANNERY . . . . .Stories, all set in the South, tend to deal with fanatics.

PARKER, DOROTHY . . . . .Frustrated love and cheated idealism presented in clever gossipy style.

POE, EDGAR ALLEN . . . . .Most well-known short story writer. Most stories create a tone of horror

PORTER, KATHERINE ANNE . . . . .Strong characters and intense emotions in well-written stories

ROTH, PHILIP . . . . .Flip, personal representations of Jewish life in the U.S.

SALINGER, J. D. . . . . .Writes about unhappy teen-age boys.

SAROYAN, WILLIAM . . . . .Stories by this Armenian who writes of the immigrant depict an optimistic search for the American Dream.

SINGER, ISAAC BASHEVIS . . . . . .Polish-born American, writes of the heritage of Polish Jews, their traditions and folkways.

STEINBECK, JOHN . . . . .Combination of realism and romance in his stories about rural people who live close to nature.

STOCKTON, FRANK . . . . .Known for both children's and adult stories that are often humorous and often deal with pseudo-science.

STUART, JESSE . . . . .Stories set in Kentucky about poor, mountain people.

THURBER, JAMES . . . . .Humorous stories usually illustrated with his humorous line drawings.

UPDIKE, JOHN . . . . .Family (sometimes dysfunctional) stories are usually set in a small Pennsylvania town.

VONNEGUT, KURT . . . . .Controversial anti-war stories, many based on his experiences in Dresden during WWII.

WALKER, ALICE . . . . .Contemporary writings about African American society.

WELTY, EUDORA . . . . .Characters, often grotesque, who fail to know themselves provide the themes for stories set in the Mississippi region.

WEST, JESSAMYN . . . . .Stories about 19th century Quaker life.

WRIGHT, RICHARD . . . . .Black author writes of racial prejudice in the South.

Figure 4.52   **The Long and the Short of It: The American Short Story**

Sample Card—Short Story Summary
(5" x 8" index card in black or blue ink)

(Front of Card)

Student's Name _____

Title of Story:	"The Tell-Tale Heart"
Author:	Edgar Allen Poe (1809-1849)
Central Character:	An unnamed younger man, whom people call mad, claims that a nervous disease has greatly sharpened his sense perceptions. He is proud of his own cleverness.
Other Characters:	The old man, whose leading feature is one pale blue, filmed eye; said to be rich, kind, and lovable. Also three policemen, not individually described.
Setting:	A shuttered house full of wind, mice, and treasures; pitch dark even in the afternoon.
Narrator:	The madman himself.
Events in summary:	(1) Dreading one vulture-like eye of the old man he shares a house with, a madman determines to kill its owner. (2) Each night he spies on the sleeping old man, but finding the eye shut, he stays his hand. (3) On the eighth night, finding the eye open, he suffocates its owner beneath the mattress and conceals the dismembered body under the floor of the bedroom. (4) Entertaining some inquiring police officers in the very room where the body lies hidden, the killer again hears (or thinks he hears) the beat of the victim's heart. (5) Terrified and convinced that the police also hear the heartbeat growing louder, the killer confesses his crime.
Tone:	Horror at the events described, skepticism toward the narrator's claims to be sane, revulsion for his gaiety and laughter.

Figure 4.52 **(continued from page 141)**

(Reverse of card)

Style:	Written as if told aloud by a deranged man eager to be believed, the story is punctuated by laughter, interjections like "Hearken," nervous halts, and fresh beginnings—indicated by dashes that grow more frequent as the story goes on and the narrator becomes more excited. Poe often relies on general adjectives ("mournful," "hideous," "hellish") to convey atmosphere; also on exact details: the lantern that emits "a single dim ray, like the thread of a spider."
Irony:	The whole story is ironic in its point-of-view. Presumably the author is not mad, nor does he enjoy the madman's self admiration, nor join in his glee. ("I then smile gaily, to find the deed so far done.") Many of the narrator's statements therefore seem verbal ironies: his account of taking an hour to move his head through the bedroom door — "Oh, you would have laughed to see how cunningly I thrust it in!" Probably we would have shuddered.
Theme:	Possibly "Murder will out," but not clearly stated or implied.
Symbols:	The vulture eye, called an Evil Eye (in superstition, one that can implant a curse), perhaps suggesting also the all-seeing eye of God the Father, from whom no guilt can be concealed. The ghostly heartbeat, sound of the victim coming back to be avenged (or the God who cannot be slain?) Deathwatches; beetles said to be death omens, whose ticking sound foreshadows the sound of the tell-tale heart "…such a sound as a watch makes when enveloped in cotton."
Evaluation:	Despite the overwrought style (to me slightly comic-bookish), a powerful story. It is an unforgettable portrait of a deranged killer. Poe knows how it is to be mad.

Figure 4.53   **The Long and the Short of It: The American Short Story**

Short Story Database

Author	Title	Source
Aiken, Conrad	"Impulse"	*Short Story Masterpieces*
	"Life Isn't a Short Story"	*The Treasury of American Short Stories*
	"Mr. Arcularis"	*Library of Great American Writing Vol. 2*
Allen, Woody	"The Kugelmass Episode"	*The Treasury of American Short Stories*
Anderson, Sherwood	"I Want to Know Why"	*Major American Short Stories*
	"I'm a Fool"	*Golden Argosy*
	"The Egg"	*The Treasury of American Short Stories*
Asimov, Isaac	Anthology available	*14 Classic Science Fiction Stories*
	Anthology available	*The Complete Robot*
	Anthology available	*The Early Asimov*
Baldwin, James	"Sonny's Blues"	*Oxford Book of American Short Stories*
	"Sonny's Blues"	*The Treasury of American Short Stories*
Barth, John	"Lost in the Funhouse"	*The Treasury of American Short Stories*
Barthelme, Donald	"Concerning the Bodyguard"	*The Treasury of American Short Stories*
Beattie, Ann	"A Reasonable Man"	*The Treasury of American Short Stories*
Bellow, Saul	"A Silver Dish"	*The Treasury of American Short Stories*
	"Looking for Mr. Green"	*Major American Short Stories*
	"Something to Remember Me By"	*Oxford Book of American Short Stories*
Benchley, Robert	"The Treasurer's Report"	*Library of Great American Writing*
	"Uncle Edith's Ghost Story"	*Russell Baker's Book of American Humor*
Benet, Stephen Vincent	"Blood of the Martyrs"	*Stories for Youth*
Bierce, Ambrose	"Parker Adderson—Philosopher"	*American Short Story Vol. 1*
	"The Coup de Grace"	*Oxford Book of Short Stories*
Boyle, Kay	"Nothing Ever Breaks Except the Heart"	*The Treasury of American Short Stories*
Bradbury, Ray	"The City"	*Science Fiction*
	"There Will Come Soft Rains"	*Oxford Book of American Short Stories*
Calisher, Hortense	"The Night Club in the Woods"	*The Treasury of American Short Stories*
Canfield, Dorothy (Fisher)	"Sex Education"	*A Treasury of Short Stories*
Capote, Truman	"A Christmas Memory"	*A Christmas Treasury*
	"A Day's Work"	*The Best of Modern Humor*
	"Children on Their Birthdays"	*The Treasury of American Short Stories*
Cather, Willa	Anthology available	*Uncle Vanya and Other Stories*
	"A Death in the Desert"	*Oxford Book of American Short Stories*
	"Neighbour Rosicky"	*The Treasury of American Short Stories*
	"Paul's Case"	*American Short Story Vol. 2*
Cheever, John	"Good-bye My Brother"	*Oxford Book of Short Stories*
	"Torch Song"	*Short Story Masterpieces*
	"Torch Song"	*The Treasury of American Short Stories*
Chopin, Kate	"A Shameful Affair"	*The Treasury of American Short Stories*
Crane, Stephen	"The Bride Comes to Yellow Sky"	*The Treasury of American Short Stories*
Dreiser, Theodore	"The Lost Phoebe"	*The Treasury of American Short Stories*
Edson, Russell	"A Man Who Writes"	*The Treasury of American Short Stories*

Figure 4.53 (continued from page 143)

Author	Title	Source
Ellison, Ralph	"Battle Royal"	*Oxford Book of American Short Stories*
	"King of the Bingo Game"	*The Treasury of American Short Stories*
Faulkner, William	Anthology available	*Faulkner Reader*
	"Barn Burning"	*Short Story Masterpieces*
	"That Evening Sun"	*The Treasury of American Short Stories*
	"The Bear"	*Great Stories from the World of Sports*
Filer, Tom	"The Last Voyage"	*The Treasury of American Short Stories*
Fitzgerald, F. Scott	Anthology available	*Bits of Paradise*
	Anthology available	*Price Was High (Last Collected Stories From ...)*
	"The Baby Party"	*The Treasury of American Short Stories*
Garrigue, Jean	"The Snowfall"	*The Treasury of American Short Stories*
Harnack, Curtis	"Voice of the Town"	*The Treasury of American Short Stories*
Harte, Bret	"The Gentleman of La Porte"	*The Treasury of American Short Stories*
Hawkes, John	"The Grandmother"	*The Treasury of American Short Stories*
Hawthorne, Nathaniel	"Rappaccini's Daughter"	*The Treasury of American Short Stories*
Hemingway, Ernest	Anthology available	*Short Stories of Ernest Hemingway*
	"Fifty Grand"	*Great Stories From the World of Sports*
	"The Killers"	*Golden Argosy*
	"The Light of the World"	*The Treasury of American Short Stories*
Hoffman, Alice C.	"Happy Families"	*The Treasury of American Short Stories*
Jackson, Shirley	"The Lottery"	*Literature*
	"The Lottery"	*The Treasury of American Short Stories*
	"The Tooth"	*Norton Book of Ghost Stories*
Jacobson, Josephine	"A Walk with Raschid"	*The Treasury of American Short Stories*
James, Henry	"The Real Thing"	*The Treasury of American Short Stories*
Jewett, Sarah Orne	"The Hiltons' Holiday"	*The Treasury of American Short Stories*
Jones, LeRoi	"The Screamers"	*The Treasury of American Short Stories*
King, Stephen	Anthology available	*Nightmares and Dreamscapes*
Lardner, Ring	"Golden Honeymoon"	*American Short Story Vol. 2*
	"Horseshoes"	*Great Stories From the World of Sports*
London, Jack	"The God of His Fathers"	*The Treasury of American Short Stories*
Malamud, Bernard	"Black is My Favorite Color"	*The Treasury of American Short Stories*
	"My Son is the Murderer"	*Oxford Book of American Short Stories*
	"The Model"	*Prize Stories-O. Henry Awards of 1984*
Mayhall, Jane	"An Old-Fashioned Story"	*The Treasury of American Short Stories*
McCullers, Carson	"The Jockey"	*The Treasury of American Short Stories*
	"The Sojourner"	*Short Story Masterpieces*
McPherson, James Alan	"A Matter of Vocabulary"	*The Treasury of American Short Stories*
Melville, Herman	"Bartleby the Scrivener"	*The Treasury of American Short Stories*
Merwin, W.S.	"Sand"	*The Treasury of American Short Stories*
O. Henry	"The World and the Door"	*The Treasury of American Short Stories*
Oates, Joyce Carol	"In the Region of Ice"	*The Treasury of American Short Stories*
	"Master Race"	*Prize Stories-O. Henry Awards of 1986*
	"Where Are You Going? Where Have You Been?"	*Vintage Book of Contemporary American Short Stories*
O'Connor, Flannery	Anthology available	*Complete Stories of Flannery O'Connor*

Figure 4.53   **(continued from page 144)**

Author	Title	Source
O'Connor, Flannery	"Parker's Back"	*Oxford Book of Short Stories*
	"Parker's Back"	*The Treasury of American Short Stories*
O'Hara, John	"One for the Road"	*The Treasury of American Short Stories*
Paley, Grace	"A Conversation with My Father"	*The Treasury of American Short Stories*
Parker, Dorothy	"A Telephone Call"	*Treasury of Short Stories*
	"Big Blonde"	*Library of Great American Writing*
	"You Were Perfectly Fine"	*The Treasury of American Short Stories*
Poe, Edgar Allan	"Ligeia"	*The Treasury of American Short Stories*
Porter, Katherine Ann	"Flowering Judas"	*Golden Argosy*
	"Jilting of Granny Weatherall"	*American Short Story Vol. 2*
	"The Grave"	*The Treasury of American Short Stories*
Potter, Nancy	"Light Timber"	*The Treasury of American Short Stories*
Powers, J.F.	"The Valiant Woman"	*The Treasury of American Short Stories*
Roth, Philip	"I Always Wanted You to Admire My Fasting"	*The Treasury of American Short Stories*
Saroyan, William	"Ancient History and Low Hurdles"	*Stories For Youth*
	"Isn't Today the Day?"	*Best American Short Stories of 1974*
	"The Daring Young Man on the Flying Trapeze"	*The Treasury of American Short Stories*
Schwartz, Delmore	"In Dreams Begin Responsibilities"	*The Treasury of American Short Stories*
Singer, Isaac Bashevis	Anthology available	*Collected Stories of Isaac Bashevis Singer*
Steinbeck, John	"Flight"	*Short Story Masterpieces*
	"Leader of the People"	*Golden Argosy*
Stockton, Frank	"Remarkable Wreck of the Thomas Hyke"	*Great Sea Stories*
	"The Lady or the Tiger?"	*Golden Argosy*
Taylor, Peter	"Three Heroines"	*The Treasury of American Short Stories*
Thurber, James	"The Secret Life of Walter Mitty"	*Russell Baker's Book of American Humor*
	"The Secret Life of Walter Mitty"	*The Treasury of American Short Stories*
	"You Can Look it Up"	*Great Stories From the World of Sports*
Twain, Mark	"The £1,000,000 Bank Note"	*The Treasury of American Short Stories*
Updike, John	"A Sandstone Farmhouse"	*Best American Short Stories of 1991*
	"Son"	*Best American Short Stories of 1974*
	"The Bulgarian Poetess"	*The Treasury of American Short Stories*
Vonnegut, Kurt	"Report on the Barnhouse Effect"	*Best of Modern Humor*
Vonnegut, Kurt, Jr.	"Welcome to the Monkey House"	*The Treasury of American Short Stories*
Walker, Alice	"Kindred Spirits"	*Prize Stories-O. Henry Awards of 1986*
	"Revenge of Hannah Kemhuff"	*Best American Short Stories of 1974*
Washington, Irving	"The Legend of Sleepy Hollow"	*The Treasury of American Short Stories*
Welty, Eudora	"A Visit of Charity"	*Oxford Book of Short Stories*
	"A Worn Path"	*The Treasury of American Short Stories*
	"Petrified Man"	*Major American Short Stories*
	"Why I Live at the P.O."	*Short Story Masterpieces*
West, Jessamyn	Anthology available	*The Friendly Persuasion*
Wharton, Edith	"After Holbein"	*The Treasury of American Short Stories*
Williams, Joy	"The Farm"	*The Treasury of American Short Stories*
Wright, Richard	"Almos' a Man"	*American Short Story Vol. 1*
	"Man Who Was Almost a Man"	*Oxford Book of American Short Stories*

Figure 4.54   **The Long and the Short of It: The American Short Story**

Student Evaluation Rubric

Note: Each card summary will be worth 100 points and will be graded on the basis of the following criteria. The total possible points for each required item are shown.

The title of the story and date of its original publication   _____ (2.5 points)

The author's name and birth and death date   _____ (2.5 points)

The name (if any) of the central character, along with a
description of that character's main traits or features.   _____ (5 points)

Other characters in the story, with a description of main
traits or features.   _____ (5 points)

A short description of the setting.   _____ (5 points)

The narrator of the story. (To identify the narrator is, of course,
to define the point-of-view from which the story is told).   _____ (5 points)

A succinct summary of the main events of the story, given in
chronological order.   _____ (15 points)

A description of the general tone of the story, as well as it can
be sensed, revealing the author's apparent feelings toward the
central character or the main events.   _____ (10 points)

Some comments on the style in which the story is written.
(Quotations are helpful if space permits.)   _____ (10 points)

If there is irony in the story, what is it and how does it
contribute to the story?   _____ (5 points)

In a sentence, the main theme of the story.   _____ (10 points)

Leading symbols of the story.   _____ (10 points)

A personal evaluation of the story as a whole from the reader's
viewpoint and group discussion and participation.   _____ (15 points)

TOTAL POINTS: _____

NOTE: Mastery of Information Skills recorded in a database with your name and skills learned.

Nobel Prize Winning Reports

Glenda Willnerd, Lincoln High School Library Media Specialist

Hilde Dale, ELL Instructor

Lincoln High School

2229 J Street, Lincoln, Nebraska 68510

402-436-1301

gwilln@lps.org

Grade Level: English Language Learners (ELL) Level 4

Unit Overview: Nobel Prize Winning Reports is a popular unit with English Language Learners. In order to aid them in their selection of a topic, students learn about Alfred Nobel and the individuals who have been selected, worldwide, to win the prestigious Nobel Prize. Students then gather and organize their information, with the aid of a graphic organizer, to write a report. Finally, they summarize the information and include it in a *PowerPoint* presentation they share with other ELL classes.

Time Frame: 3 weeks

Content Area Standards: Lincoln Public Schools English Language Learner Goals and Standards: *Draft form. *ESL Standards for Pre-K-12 Students*. Alexandria: Teachers of English to Speakers of Other Languages, Inc., 1997.

ELL Goal II: To use English to achieve academically in all content areas.

Standard 1: Students will use English to interact in the classroom.

Objective: ELL Level 4 – Begin to present oral reports using only notes or cue card support.

Standard 2: Students will use English to obtain, process, construct, and provide subject matter information in spoken and written form.

Objective: ELL Level 4 – Begin to write a multi-paragraph response in which ideas, sentences, and paragraphs are organized and connected.

Objective: ELL Level 4 – Write a report using at least three media sources.

Objective: ELL Level 4 – Summarize important ideas of level-appropriate materials.

Standard 3: Students will use appropriate learning strategies to construct and apply academic knowledge.

Objective: ELL Level 4 – Use media resources to find and present information and accurately cite sources.

Objective: ELL Level 4 – Take notes independently within a teacher-generated framework.

Content Area Standards: Nebraska Reading/Writing Standards

<http://www.nde.state.ne.us/READ/Standards/ReadingWritingStandards.htm>

12.1 Reading

12.1.1 By the end of twelfth grade, students will identify the basic facts and essential ideas in what they have read or viewed.

Student demonstrations:

- Demonstrate comprehension through written and oral responses.

12.1.2 By the end of twelfth grade, students will locate, access, and evaluate resources to identify appropriate information.

Student demonstrations:

- Extend the use of electronic and print reference resources to meet information needs, including the use of such resources as gazetteers, atlases, specialized indexes, bibliographies, periodicals, handbooks, manuals, government documents, books of quotations, and college and career resources.
- Use electronic resources such as CD-ROM and online resources.
- Use software programs, such as word processing and multimedia presentation tools, to synthesize and present information.
- Use other library resources to select reading materials and resources of interest.
- Identify and gather resources that provide relevant and reliable information for research projects.

12.1.6 By the end of twelfth grade, students will read, identify, analyze, and apply knowledge of the structure, elements, and meaning of nonfiction or informational material and provide evidence from the text to support their understanding.

Student demonstrations:

- Analyze and describe the structure and elements of biographical and other nonfictional works.

12.2 Writing

12.2.1 By the end of twelfth grade, students will identify, describe, and apply knowledge of the structure of the English language and standard English conventions for sentence structure, usage, punctuation, capitalization, and spelling.

Student demonstrations:

- Apply all conventions of standard English to writing.

12.2.2 By the end of the twelfth grade, students will write compositions with a clear focus, logically related ideas, and adequate supporting detail.

Student demonstrations:

- Write compositions with a clear focus, adequate detail, and well-developed paragraphs.
- Evaluate the effectiveness of the strategies they use to generate and organize their ideas.

12.2.3 By the end of the twelfth grade, students will demonstrate improvement in organization, content, word choice, voice, sentence fluency and standard English conventions after revising and editing their compositions.

Student demonstrations:

- Revise their writing to improve voice, word choice, sentence fluency, and subtlety of meaning after rethinking how well they have addressed questions of purpose, audience, and genre.
- Use all conventions of standard English in their writing across the curriculum.
- Individually develop, explain, and use criteria for assessing their own composition work across the curriculum.

12.2.5 Students will use self-generated questions, note taking, summarizing, and outlining to enhance learning.

Student demonstrations:

- Use their own summaries, notes, and outlines in writing research papers.

12.3 Speaking
12.3.2 By the end of the twelfth grade, students will make oral presentations that demonstrate appropriate consideration of audience, purpose, and information to be conveyed.
Student demonstrations:
- Use multimedia to deliver formal presentations.

Information Power Information Literacy Standards and Indicators: 1.1, 1.2, 1.4, 1.5, 2.1, 2.2, 2.3, 2.4, 3.1, 3.4, 5.3, 6.1, 7.1, 7.2, 8.2, 8.3, 9.1, 9.2

Cooperative Teaching Plan:

Library Media Specialist Will:
- Prepare thumbnail sketches of Nobel Prize winners around the world from which students will choose their topics.
- Create a graphic organizer for students to use as they gather information.
- Gather resources and model for students how to access information in each resource.
- Demonstrate recording of bibliographic information and citing resources using MLA documentation style.
- Instruct students in creation of a *PowerPoint* presentation
- Collaborate with the classroom teacher and students to create rubrics for the research process, the written report, and the *PowerPoint* presentation.
- Assist in the assessment of the *PowerPoint* presentation.

Teacher Will:
- Assign a reading on Alfred Nobel and Nobel Prize winners as homework to prepare students for this unit.
- Assist students as they select Nobel Prize winners for their topics.
- Assist students as they gather information from both print and electronic resources.
- Edit rough draft of written report.
- Collaborate with the library media specialist and students to create rubrics for the research process, the written report, and the *PowerPoint* presentation.
- Use rubrics to assess students written reports and *PowerPoint* presentation.

Resources:

Print
A wide variety of individual biographies of Nobel Prize winners.

McGrayne, Sharon Bertsch. *Nobel Prize Women in Science: Their Lives, Struggles, and Momentous Discoveries*. Secaucus: Carol Publishing, 1992.

Meyer, Edith Patterson. *In Search of Peace: The Winners of the Nobel Peace Prize 1901-1975*. Nashville: Abingdon, 1978.

Nobel Prize Winners: An H.W. Wilson Biographical Dictionary. New York: H.W. Wilson, 1987.

Schraff, Anne E. *Women of Peace: Nobel Peace Prize Winners*. Berkeley Heights: Enslow Publishers, 1994.

The Who's Who of Nobel Prize Winners. Phoenix: Oryx Press, 1991.

World Book Encyclopedia. Chicago: World Book, Inc., 2000.

Electronic

Discovering Collection
> <http://galenet.galegroup.com>. (Requires subscription)

The Nobel Prize Internet Archive. 24 July 2002
> <http://nobelprizes.com>.

Wilson Biographies Plus Illustrated
> <http://hwwilsonweb.com>. (Requires subscription)

Equipment

Computer and video projector

Product or Culminating Activity: Students write a report and create a *PowerPoint* presentation with a minimum of seven slides on their Nobel Prize winner. The audience for this presentation will be other ELL classes.

Assessment Overview: The process, the paper, and the *PowerPoint* presentation are assessed by the classroom teacher using three rubrics, with the assistance of the library media specialist on the *PowerPoint* assessment.

Figure 4.55 **Nobel Prize Winning Reports**

Graphic Organizer

1. Question

Briefly, who is this person and why is this person important?
notes:
introduction
summary
picture

2. Question

Tell about this person's early life and education.
notes:
paragraph
summary
picture

3. Question

Tell about this person's educational background and accomplishments.
notes:
paragraph
summary
picture

4. Question

What did this person do to win the Nobel Prize?
notes:
paragraph
summary
picture

5. Question

Discuss what other aspect of this person's life is important.
notes
paragraph
summary
picture

6. Question

What are your reactions and what is your opinion about this person?
notes:
conclusion
summary
picture

Figure 4.56	Nobel Prize Winning Reports

Process Rubric

1. Topic	Quality		Acceptable		Not Included
	4	3	2	1	0
selects topic					
identifies key words					
or related words					

2. Question Quality	Quality		Acceptable		Not Included
	4	3	2	1	0
writes questions					
independently					

3. Resources	Quality		Acceptable		Not Included
	4	3	2	1	0
identifies and locates					
resources independently					

4. Notetaking	Quality		Acceptable		Not Included
	4	3	2	1	0
paraphrases – takes notes					
using own words					

5. Organization	Quality		Acceptable		Not Included
	4	3	2	1	0
introduction					
sequences information					
conclusion					

6. Evaluation	Quality		Acceptable		Not Included
	4	3	2	1	0
process					
product					

Figure 4.57   **Nobel Prize Winning Reports**

Paper Rubric

1. Title Page

	Quality		Acceptable		Not Included
	4	3	2	1	0
topic					
student's name					
date completed					
picture (optional)					

2. Paper

	Quality		Acceptable		Not Included
	4	3	2	1	0
typed (1-2 pages)					
student's name					
double-spaced					
font - size 14					

3. Paragraphs

	Quality		Acceptable		Not Included
	4	3	2	1	0
topic sentence					
supporting details					

4. Mechanics

	Quality		Acceptable		Not Included
	4	3	2	1	0
spelling					
grammar					
punctuation					

5. Works Cited

	Quality		Acceptable		Not Included
	4	3	2	1	0
MLA format					
alphabetical order					

Figure 4.58   **Nobel Prize Winning Reports**

PowerPoint Rubric

1. Design	Quality		Acceptable		Not Included
	4	3	2	1	0
introduction					
body					
conclusion					
slides relate to the text					
slides show design elements and use of creativity					

2. Content	Quality		Acceptable		Not Included
	4	3	2	1	0
accurate					
interesting and arranged in sequence					
correct grammar, punctuation and spelling					

3. Presentation	Quality		Acceptable		Not Included
	4	3	2	1	0
well-prepared					
speaks clearly and easy to understand					
looks at audience					
uses good posture					

Out of this World Sports

Dr. Lesley S. J. Farmer, Associate Professor
California State University Long Beach
1250 Bellflower Blvd., Long Beach, California 90840
562-985-4509
lfarmer@csulb.edu

Grade Level: 9-12

Unit Overview: In Out of this World Sports, students reconfigure games for play on other planets. In groups of five, they choose a sport and research its rules and its physical aspects, such as projectiles, speed, and weight issues. After regrouping in jigsaw fashion, they research planet characteristics such as gravity, atmosphere, and surface to determine the accommodations that must be made in order to play the game on that planet. Individually, each student analyzes his/her sport in terms of the properties of the planet and identifies the necessary accommodations for play on that planet. This activity may be used in mathematics, science, and physical education courses.

Time Frame: Three hours of library time

Content Area Standards: Content Standards for California Public Schools
<http://www.cde.ca.gov/standards/>

Science Content Standards, Grades 9-12

Earth Sciences: Earth's Place in the Universe
1. Astronomy and planetary exploration reveal the solar system's structure, scale, and change over time.
   a. Students know how the differences and similarities among the sun, the terrestrial planets, and the gas planets may have been established during the formation of the solar system.

Investigation and Experimentation
1. Scientific progress is made by asking meaningful questions and conducting careful investigations. As a basis for understanding this concept and addressing the content in the other four strands, students should develop their own questions and conduct their own investigations.
   a. Select and use appropriate tools and technology (such as computer-linked probes, spread sheets, and graphing calculators) to perform tests, collect data, analyze relationships, and display data.
   e. Solve scientific problems by using quadratic equations and simple trigonometric, exponential, and logarithmic functions.
   i. Analyze situations and solve problems that require combining and applying concepts from more than one area of science.

Physics: Motion and Forces

1. Newton's laws predict the motion of most objects.
   a. Students know how to solve problems that involve constant speed and average speed.
   f. Students know applying a force to an object perpendicular to the direction of its motion causes the object to change direction but not speed.
   i. Students know how to solve two-dimensional trajectory problems.

Information Power Information Literacy Standards and Indicators: 1.1, 1.2, 1.3, 1.4, 1.5, 2.1, 2.2, 2.4, 3.1, 3.2, 3.3, 3.4, 6.2, 8.3, 9.1, 9.2, 9.3, 9.4

Cooperative Teaching Plan:

Library Media Specialist Will:

■ Facilitate student research strategy decisions. Guiding questions include:
- How important is current information?
- Where would it be found?
- In what subject areas would information be found?

■ Help students to locate and evaluate information sources as needed.

Teacher Will:

■ Introduce activity. The essential question is:
- How do the physical properties of a planet affect sports played there?

■ Lead a class discussion on planet features: dimensions, distance from the sun, rotation, temperature, atmosphere, topology, etc.

■ Lead a class discussion on elements of sports: dimensions of playing fields, actions (projecting objects, body motion, collisions, etc.)

■ Lead a class discussion on possible ways that a planet's features would affect how a sport is played. For instance:
- How does gravity affect projectiles and body movement?
- How does atmosphere affect breathing or corrosion?
- How does temperature affect objects and human bodies?

■ Assign groups of five and coordinate group choices of sports and planets.

■ Help students analyze physics principles as applied to various sports.

■ Assess student work using rubrics.

Resources:

Print

Bakich, Michael E. *The Cambridge Planetary Handbook.* Cambridge, Massachusetts: Cambridge University Press, 2000.

Bond, Peter. *DK Guide to Space.* New York: Dorling Kindersley, 1999.

Bloomfield, Louise A. *How Things Work: The Physics of Everyday Life.* New York: Wiley, 1997.

Brancazio, Peter J. *SportsScience: Physical Laws and Optimal Performance.* New York: Simon & Schuster, 1984.

Branley, Franklin. *The Planets in Our Solar System.* New York: HarperCollins. 1998.

Fortin, Francois, ed. Sports: *The Complete Visual Reference.* Buffalo, New York: Firefly, 2000.

Macaulay, David. *The New Way Things Work.* Boston: Houghton Mifflin, 1998.

McNab, David. *The Planets.* New Haven, Connecticut: Yale University Press, 1999.

Parker, Steve. *How the Body Works.* Pleasantville, New York: Reader's Digest Association, 1994.

Schrier, Eric W. and William F. Allman, eds. *Newton at the Bat.* rev. ed. New York: Scribner & Sons, 1984.

Sports Rules on File. New York: Facts on File, 2000.

Whitfield, Philip, ed. *The Human Body Explained.* New York: Holt, 1995.

Zumerchik, John, ed. *Encyclopedia of Sports Science.* New York: Macmillan, 1997.

Electronic

AllSports: Sports Central. 24 July 2002
        <http://www.allsports.com>.

Beyond Earth. 24 July 2002
        <http://www.wilders.force9.co.uk/BeyondEarth/>.

Exploratorium. 624 July 2002
        <http://www.exploratorium.edu>.

"Extrasolar Planets Encyclopedia." *Observatoire de Paris.* 14 March 2002. 24 July 2002
        <http://www.obspm.fr/planets>.

Hamilton, Calvin J. *Views of the Solar System.* 24 July 2002
<http://www.solarviews.com/eng/homepage.htm>.

How Things Work. 17 June 2002. 24 July 2002
        <http://howthingswork.virginia.edu/>.

Marshall Brian's How Stuff Works. 24 July 2002
        <http://www.howstuffworks.com/>.

NASA Education Program. 24 July 2002. 24 July 2002
        <http://education.nasa.gov>.

The Nine Planets. 27 February 2001. 24 July 2002
        <http://www.nineplanets.org/>.

"NOVA Online." *PBS.* 24 July 2002
        < http://www.pbs.org/wgbh/nova/>.

"Solar System." *KidsAstronomy.* 24 July 2002
        <http://www.kidsastronomy.com/solar_system.htm>.

Sports Media: Sports Links. 25 July 2002. 25 July 2002
        <http://www.sports-media.org>.

Weisstein, Eric. "Eric Weisstein's Treasure Trove of Astronomy." *Eric Weisstein's Treasure Trove of Science.* 24 July 2002. 24 July 2002
        < http://www.treasure-troves.com/astro/>.

"Welcome to the Planets." *NASA Planetary Data System.* 24 July 2002
        <http://pds.jpl.nasa.gov/planets/welcome.htm>.

"Yahoo: Sports." *Yahoo.* 24 July 2002
        <http://www.yahoo.com/Recreation/Sports/>.

Equipment

posterboard, writing instruments, presentation software, etc.

Product or Culminating Activity: Students will create a poster (alternatively an electronic presentation) showing how to play the selected sport on the selected planet with modifications.

Assessment Overview: Activity is assessed with both a process and a product rubric. Overall critical points of assessment include: scientific soundness of the information, mathematical rigor of the calculations, thoroughness and accuracy of the information and the analysis, quality of collaboration, and quality of the presentation/poster.

Adaptations and Extensions: Other activities on planets (e.g., eating, work, etc.)
Sports adaptations in different biomes or at different altitudes on Earth
Sports adaptations due to differences in bodies (e.g., age, gender, fitness, etc.)

Figure 4.59 **Out of this World Sports**

Research Product Evaluation Rubric

	Adherence to Assignment	Organization	Proof and Justification: Commentary	Use of Language and Strategies	Spelling and Grammar
6	All aspects of the assignment covered in depth. Bibliography and citations done according to format without errors. Assignment is free of plagiarism.	Well-organized structure & paragraphs that support an insightful and defined thesis.	Substantial & appropriate proof with convincing justification & commentary.	Language is mature and clear, and sentence structure is varied and well developed.	Errors are rare.
5	All aspects of the assignment covered. Bibliography and citations done according to format with few or no errors. Assignment is free of plagiarism.	Organized structure & paragraphs that support a clearly defined thesis.	Suitable proof with convincing justification & commentary.	Language is effective and clear, and sentence structure is somewhat varied.	Errors are infrequent.
4	Most aspects of the assignment covered. Bibliography and citations done according to format with occasional errors. Assignment is free of plagiarism.	Paragraphs and organization give support to a simplistic thesis.	Adequate proof with somewhat convincing justification & commentary.	Language is adequate and clear, and sentence structure is somewhat varied.	Errors appear occasionally.
3	Several important aspects of the assignment are missing. Bibliography and citations contain frequent and distracting errors. Assignment is free of plagiarism.	Unorganized structure and paragraphs with an under-developed or vague thesis.	Inadequate proof with underdeveloped or vague justification & commentary.	Language is awkward, and sentence structure is simplistic.	Errors appear often and distract the reader.
2	Many important aspects of the assignment are missing. Bibliography and citations incomplete. Assignment may contain uncited information.	Unorganized structure & paragraphs with no apparent-thesis or focus.	Inadequate proof with little clear or related justification or commentary.	Language is unclear or repetitive, and sentence structure is simplistic and lacks control.	Errors appear continuously and distract the reader.
1	Most important aspects of the assignment are missing. Bibliography and citations missing or incomplete. Assignment contains plagiarism.	No organization is present, and paper lacks thesis.	Clearly lacking proof with little or no justification or commentary, or unrelated commentary.	Language is ineffective or repetitive, and sentence structure is simplistic and lacks control.	Errors are numerous and distract the reader.

Figure 4.60   **Out of this World Sports**

Research Process Evaluation Rubric

TARGET INDICATORS	1 Emerging	2 Nearly Proficient	3 Accomplished	4 Exceptional
I. Determines information needs	*Someone else defines the topic and what. information I need.	*Someone else defines the topic. I can identify, with help, some of the information I need.	*I detemine a topic and identify the information I need.	*I detemine a manageable topic and identify the kinds of information I need to support it.
II. Develops search strategy	*Someone else selects the resources I need and shows me how to find the information. *Someone also develops my plan and timeline. *I don't know what to record.	*I select resources but they aren't always appropriate. *I have an incomplete plan and a timeline, but don't always stick to them. *I return to the same source to find bibliographic details.	*I use a variety of information strategies and resources. *I have a complete plan and stay on my timeline. *I sometimes record bibliographic information.	*I always select appropriate strategies and resources. *I have a complete plan and can adjust my timeline when needed. *I always record bibliographic information for all my sources.
III. Locates and accesses sources	*I don't understand how to use information resources.	*I don't use a variety of information resources.	*I prefer to limit the number of information resources I use.	*I am comfortable using various information resources.
IV. Accesses and comprehends information	*Someone else helps me extract details from sources. *I have no way to determine what information to keep and what to discard.	*I can extract details and concepts from one type of information resource. *I sometimes apply appropriate criteria to decide which information to use.	*I extract details and concepts from different types of resources. *I examine my information and apply criteria to decide what to use.	*I extract details and concepts from all types of resources. *I effectively apply criteria to decide what information to use.

Figure 4.60 (continued from page 160)

TARGET INDICATORS	1 Emerging	2 Nearly Proficient	3 Accomplished	4 Exceptional
V. Interprets and organizes information	*I need help finding which sources to use. I don't know how to use facts. *I have trouble processing and organizing information. *I need to be reminded to credit sources.	*I use the minimum number of sources assigned. I can use 1–2 very well. *I know some ways to organize information. I just list the facts. *Sometimes I credit sources appropriately.	*I create and improve my product by using a variety of resources from school. *I organize information in different ways. *I usually credit sources appropriately.	*I compare/contrast facts from a variety of resources found both in and out of my community. I use various media for products and audiences. *I organize information needs. *I always credit sources appropriately.
VI. Communicates the information	*I'm not sure what actions to take based on my information needs. *My product is incomplete. I don't revise.	*I know what to do with the information I find. *I complete my product, but need help revising.	*I act based on the information I have processed, according to my needs. *I complete, practice, and revise my product.	*I act independently on the relevent information I have processed, and explain my actions clearly. *I complete, practice, and revise my product several times. I ask for feedback.
VII. Evaluates product and process	*I don't know how well I did. I need someone to help me figure out how to improve.	*I know how well I did, and have some idea of how to improve.	*I know how well I did, and make some revisions.	*I evaluate the product and process throughout my work, and revise when needed.

Political Parties—Then and Now

Penny Arnold, Librarian
Rob Finkill, Eighth Grade American Cultures Teacher
Hershey Middle School
Homestead Road, Hershey, Pennsylvania 17033
717-531-2222
parnold@hershey.k12.pa.us

Grade Level: 8

Unit Overview: Political Parties—Then and Now provides students with an opportunity to explore the platforms of political parties of the past and present. Research topics include the Democrat-Republicans, 1792-1817; the Federalists, 1787-1820; the Democratic Republicans, 1826-1828; the Democratic Party, 1828-present; the National Republican Party, 1826-1834; the Whig Party, 1834-1854; and the Republican Party, 1854-present. Platforms and influential people are highlighted. Groups publish a booklet based upon their research. Additionally, using information located about current political parties, each student will determine the party's position on school uniforms. Positions may be presented in a variety of formats, but will include a short oral presentation.

Time Frame: Two weeks in classroom and library

Content Area Standards: Proposed Academic Standards for Civics and Government, Pennsylvania Department of Education
<http:www.pde.state.pa.us/k12/lib/k12/civics.pdf>

Civics and Government, Middle and High
5.2 Rights and Responsibilities of Citizenship
5.2.9.C. Analyze skills used to resolve conflicts in society and government.

5.3 How Government Works
5.3.6.E. Identify major leaders of local, state and national governments, their primary duties and their political party affiliation.
5.3.9.A. Explain the structure, organization and operation of the local, state and national governments including domestic and national policy-making.
5.3.9.E. Explain how citizens participate in choosing their leaders throughout political parties, campaigns and elections.

Content Area Standards: Proposed Academic Standards for History, Pennsylvania Department of Education
<http:www.pde.state.pa.us/k12/lib/k12/histwhole.pdf>

8.2 Pennsylvania History

8.2.9 Analyze the political and cultural contributions of individuals and groups to Pennsylvania history from 1787 to 1914.

8.3 United States History

8.3.9.A Identify and analyze the political and cultural contributions of individuals and groups to United States history from 1787 to 1914.

8.3.9.B Identify and analyze primary documents, material artifacts and historic sites important in United States history from 1787 to 1914.

8.3.9.C Analyze how continuity and change has influenced United States history from 1787 to 1914.

Content Area Standards: Academic Standards for Reading, Writing, Speaking and Listening, Pennsylvania Department of Education <http://www.pde.state.pa.us/k12/lib/k12/Reading.pdf>

1.1 Learning to Read Independently

1.1.8.A Locate appropriate texts for an assigned purpose before reading.

1.1.8.D Identify basic facts and ideas in text using specific strategies.

1.1.8.G Demonstrate after reading understanding and interpretation of both fiction and nonfiction text, including public documents.

1.1.8.G.4 Describe the context of a document.

1.2 Reading Critically in All Content Areas

1.2.8.A Read and understand essential content of informational texts and documents in all academic areas.

1.2.8.A.1 Differentiate fact from opinion utilizing resources that go beyond traditional text.

1.2.8.A.2 Distinguish between essential and nonessential information across texts and going beyond texts to a variety of media; identify bias and propaganda where present.

1.2.8.A.3 Draw inferences based on a variety of information sources.

1.2.8.A.4 Evaluate text organization and content to determine the author's purpose and effectiveness according to the author's theses, accuracy and thoroughness.

1.4 Types of Writing

1.4.8.B Write multi-paragraph information pieces.

1.4.8.C Write persuasive pieces.

1.4.8.C.2 Include convincing, elaborated and properly cited evidence.

1.5 Quality of Writing

1.5.8.A Write with a sharp, distinct focus.

1.5.8.A.1 Identify topic, task and audience.

1.5.8.A.2 Establish a single point of view.

1.5.8.B Write using well-developed content appropriate for the topic.

1.5.8.B.2 Employ the most effective format for the purpose and audience.

1.5.8.B.3 Write paragraphs that have details and information specific to the topic and relevant to the focus.

1.6 Speaking and Listening

1.6.8.A Listen to others.

1.6.8.D Contribute to discussions.

1.6.8.E Participate in small and large group discussions and presentations.

1.8 Research

1.8.8.B Locate information using appropriate sources and strategies.

1.8.8.B.1 Determine valid resources for researching the topic, including primary and secondary sources.

1.8.8.B.2 Evaluate the importance and quality of the sources.

1.8.8.B.3 Select essential sources.

1.8.8.B.4 Use table of contents, indices, key words, cross-references and appendices.

1.8.8.B.5 Use traditional and electronic search tools.

1.8.8.C Organize, summarize and present the main ideas from research.

1.8.8.C.5 Use formatting techniques to create an understandable presentation for designated audience.

Content Area Standards: Academic Standards for Science and Technology, Pennsylvania Department of Education <http://www.pde.state.pa.us/k12/lib/k12/scitech.pdf>

3.7.7.C Explain and demonstrate basic computer operations and concepts.

3.7.7.D Apply computer software to solve specific problems.

3.7.7.E Explain basic computer communication systems.

Information Power Information Literacy Standards and Indicators: 1.1, 1.2, 1.3, 1.4, 1.5, 2.1, 2.2, 2.3, 2.4, 3.1, 3.2, 3.3, 3.4, 6.1, 6.2, 9.1, 9.2, 9.3, 9.4

Cooperative Teaching Plan:

Librarian Will:

■ Instruct students in and reinforce the following skills:
  - Use of OPAC search strategies using Power search and Boolean operators.
  - Use of POWER Library resources, including the EBSCO periodical database utilizing either print or e-mail feature and Access PA interloan database.
  - Use of *Gale Junior Reference* online resource print or email features.
  - Internet searches with a focus on string searching, evaluation of Web addresses, and evaluation of information.
  - Correct bibliographical citations.
  - Recognizing the differences between biases, opinions, and factual information.

■ Monitor and assist students in locating, analyzing, and applying information.

■ Correct bibliographies following the *Hershey Middle School Writer's Guide*.

Teacher Will:

■ Introduce each political party to be researched by providing a brief overview.

■ Introduce a variety of influential members of each political party.

■ Explain the scope of the project to students.

■ Monitor and assist students in locating, analyzing, and applying information.

■ Explain and present a variety of forms used to express opinions to political leaders, such as letters, posters, or commercials.

■ Present topic of interest to students—school uniforms—to stimulate interest and discussion of "point of view" of political parties.

■ Assess historical and present day projects using Grading Sheets with attention to: focus, content, organization, style, conventions, and group dynamics.

Resources:

Print

Academic American. Danbury, Connecticut: Grolier, 1998.

Binkley, Wilfred Ellsworth. *American Political Parties; Their Natural History.* New York: Knopf, 1962.

Clements, John. *Chronology of the United States.* Dallas, Texas: Political Research, 1997.

Collier, Christopher and James Lincoln Collier. *Building a New Nation: The Federalist Era, 1789-1801.* New York: Benchmark Books, 1999.

Collier, Christopher and James Lincoln Collier. *The Jeffersonian Republican: The Louisiana Purchase and the War of 1812, 1800-1823.* New York: Benchmark, 1999.

Delury, George E. *World Encyclopedia of Political Systems and Parties.* New York: Facts on File, 1987.

Encyclopedia Americana. Danbury, Connecticut: Grolier, 1997.

Frank, Beryl. *Pictorial History of the Republican Party.* Secaucus, New Jersey: Castle Books, 1980.

Kronenwetler, Michael. *Political Parties of the United States.* Berkley Heights, New Jersey: Enslow, 1996.

Morin, Isobel V. *Politics, American Style: Political Parties in American History.* Brookfield, Connecticut: Millbrook Press, 1999.

Moss, Joyce and George Wilson. *Profiles in America History.* Detroit: Gale Research, 1994.

National Party Conventions, 1831-1992. Washington, D.C.: Congressional Quarterly, 1995.

New Book of Knowledge. Danbury, Connecticut: Grolier, 1995.

O'Brien, Steven G. *American Political Leaders from Colonial Times to the Present.* Santa Barbara: ABC-CLIO, 1991.

Taylor, L. B. *The New Right.* New York: Franklin Watts, 1981.

World Book Encyclopedia. Chicago: World Book, 2000.

Electronic

"About Our Party." *Republican National Committee.* 24 July 2002
< http://www.rnc.org/gopinfo>.

Andrew, Joe. "The Democratic Party." *Democratic National Committee.* 24 July 2002
<http://www.democrats.org/about>.

Gale Junior Reference Collection. Gale Research. (Requires subscription)

Lee, Roger A. "The History of American Political Parties." *The History Guy.* 1 October 2000.
25 July 2002
<http://www.historyguy.com/party_histories.html>.

Note: The POWER Library is a service to Pennsylvania's public libraries, school libraries and the State Library. It allows access to thousands of full text periodical articles, newspapers, a major encyclopedia, plus photographs, pictures, charts, maps, reference materials for young people and more. The databases to be used for this project include but are not limited to: EBSCO, Searchasaurus, SIRS Discoverer, and Access PA.

Product or Culminating Activity: Students will be responsible for two projects. The first will be creation of a booklet describing and illustrating the parties' platforms and people influential in the formation of the political parties of the past. The second project involves applying knowledge of current political parties to state the position on the issue of school uniforms in the form of a letter, a diary or journal entry, a poster, a poem, a commercial, a bumper sticker, or a skit.

Assessment Overview: The Social Studies teacher and the librarian will evaluate the accuracy of research, the quality of writing, using the Pennsylvania Writing Assessment Domain Scoring Guide, group participation, creativeness, and presentation quality.

Extension: Gifted students may be asked to write and word process a letter, in correct business letter format, stating their feelings regarding a current event topic of their choice to the State Senator and Congressman.

Figure 4.61   **Political Parties—Then and Now**

Projects Overview

You will be doing research on the political parties of the past and the present to determine what they thought and stood for in the past and what they think and stand for now.

Your group will do research on the following parties:
- ◆ Democrat-Republicans, 1792–1817
- ◆ Federalists, 1787–1820
- ◆ Democratic Republicans, 1826–1828
- ◆ Democratic Party, 1828–present
- ◆ National Republican Party, 1826–1834
- ◆ Whig Party, 1834–1854
- ◆ Republican Party, 1854–present

Consider explicit information when you are researching—the who?, what?, why?, where?, when? and how? For example: Consider whether the party's platform included/includes strong federal or state government control. Is the party still in existence? Why or why not?

PROJECTS

HISTORICAL PROJECT - 100 Points:
1. Create a booklet describing and/or illustrating the platforms of each party and the people influential in the formation of these political parties.
2. Each group will make ONE booklet. Determine group roles and jobs to complete the task.
3. Computer time will be available to complete the publication.
4. The project will be assessed on: focus, content, organization, style, conventions, and group participation.

PRESENT DAY PROJECT - 100 Points:
1. After randomly selecting a political party, use what you know about the current political parties to state that party's position on SCHOOL UNIFORMS.
2. You may chose to present the position in the form of a letter to an editor or Congressman, a diary or journal entry, a poster, a poem, a commercial, or a skit. Other choices may be discussed with your teacher.
3. During a short presentation, you will present your project to the class.
4. The project will be assessed on: focus, content, organization, style, conventions, and presentation.

Figure 4.62 **Political Parties—Then and Now**

Keyword Search Plan

It is always wise to have a plan before you begin your research. Brainstorm major ideas and concepts using the Boolean operator "and". Consider all of the related terms or synonyms to assist in your search.

Major Topic		

Subtopics		

Synonym	Synonym	Synonym

Figure 4.63   Political Parties—Then and Now

Compare and Contrast Outline

Idea 1:	Idea 2:

How Alike?

How Different?

	Issue 1	
	Issue 2	
	Issue 3	
	Issue 4	

Conclusion:

| Figure 4.64 | Political Parties—Then and Now |

ABCD'S Checklist for Web Page Evaluation

Web page: _____

URL: _____

AUTHOR:

Who is responsible for creating/maintaining the page? _____

What are his/her qualifications? _____

Is there an e-mail address included on the page? _____

_____

The author is associated with: ___K–12 school ___University ___Government agency ___Organization ___Company ___Other

ACCURACY:

Where did the originator get the materials?_____
Can the sources be verified? _____
Is the source credited on the page? ___Yes ___No
Does the information appear to be accurate? ___Yes ___No
Are there errors in spelling, grammar, or links? ___Yes ___No

BIAS:

What is the purpose for the information being there? Check all that apply.
___ Research information ___ Links to related information ___ Student projects
___ Questions and answers ___ Communication with experts ___ Teacher materials
___ Interactivities ___ Multimedia elements ___ Graphics
___ Advertisements ___ Opinion/editorial ___ Other
Is there a bias or point of view? ___Yes ___No
Please describe:

CURRENCY:

When was the page created? _____
When was the most recent update? _____
Is any information out of date? ___Yes ___No

| **Figure 4.64** | **(continued from page 172)** |

DETAIL:

Check the information for details. Look at the table of contents, graphics, and headings. Will it be useful for your project? ___Yes ___No

Are links provided to additional sites? ___Yes ___No

Are those links useful? ___Yes ___No

Are those links still active? ___Yes ___No

Is the information a primary or secondary source or a combination?

_____

Could you have gotten the information elsewhere? ___Yes ___No

If yes, which print or non-print sources would have worked as well?

_____

DOMAINS:

Under what domain is the document posted?
.com ___ .edu ___ .gov ___ .mil ___ .net ___ .org ___

Is there additional information available in the URL? For example, if it is an "edu site," can you determine what type of educational site (k12, university, etc.)?

_____

Can you tell the country of origin? (.us, .au. .uk, etc.)

_____

Is there anything else you can determine?

_____

Figure 4.65   Political Parties—Then and Now

Historical Project Grading Sheet

This form will be used to grade your group's historical information.

FOCUS	_____/20

Booklet tells specifically what each party represented.
Booklet zeros in on the important information.
During work time, your group worked hard and stayed on task.

CONTENT	_____/20

Information provided is accurate and informative.
All areas are complete.
Each page is high quality work.

ORGANIZATION	_____/20

Booklet follows the table of contents.
Organization is logical and makes sense.
Time and care is shown in final product.

STYLE	_____/10

Creative and unique ideas are used.
Ideas are original, not copied.

CONVENTIONS	_____/10

Grammar, mechanics, spelling, usage and sentence formation
are all correct.

GROUP PARTICIPATION	_____/20

This will be an individual grade, based on your input, input from your group, and input from your
teacher and your librarian. (See Group Evaluation sheet)

TOTAL	_____/100

(This score may differ from that of other members of your group
because of the group participation grade.)

Figure 4.66   **Political Parties—Then and Now**

Present Day Project Grading Sheet

This form will be used to grade your presentation of current information on the following areas:

PRESENTATION OF YOUR SIDE _____/25

You showed accurately how your party would feel about the school uniforms issue using real examples.

OPPONENTS' SIDE REFUTED _____/25

You explained how your opposition would see the issue, but showed how it was incorrect according to your platform.

INFORMATION _____/20

Information presented was relevant and accurate according to the party's beliefs.
You helped the class clearly see their side of the issue.

STRENGTH OF PRESENTATION _____/40

You did a great job.
We understood what you were trying to say.
You stated your position in a creative and informative way.
You were well prepared and it was evident you practiced.
It was clear to all who were listening.
Your audience was attentive.

TOTAL _____/100

Figure 4.67   **Political Parties—Then and Now**

Group and Self Evaluation

On this form evaluate yourself and your group members. Be honest in your evaluation of the work both you and other group members did.

Personal Evaluation:
List the work you did on the booklet.

_____

_____

_____

_____

_____

_____

_____

My score for myself:	5	10	15	20
Teacher score for me:	5	10	15	20
Librarian score for me:	5	10	15	20

Evaluation of Group Member:

Name _____	5	10	15	20
Name _____	5	10	15	20
Name _____	5	10	15	20
Name _____	5	10	15	20

Politics and *PowerPoint*: Bringing Julius Caesar into the 21st Century

Jo Ann Wahrman, Librarian

Sharon Palmquist, English Teacher

Goodland High School

P. O. Box 509, Goodland, Kansas 67735

785-899-5656

jwahrman@kweb.net

Grade Level: 10

Unit Overview: Politics and PowerPoint introduces students to biographical library references while they research victims of political assassinations throughout history as a pre-activity to reading *Julius Caesar*. Students take notes, create a bibliography of all sources used, organize the material, and submit the organized information to the rest of the class in an oral presentation using *PowerPoint*. Final assessment utilizes a set of rubrics.

Time Frame: 2 weeks

Content Area Standards: Kansas Curriculum Standards for Reading and Writing
   <http://www.ksde.org/outcomes/communications.html>

Communication, Secondary

Standard 1: Learners demonstrate skill in reading a variety of materials for a variety of purposes.

Benchmark 1: The proficient reader comprehends whole pieces of narration, exposition, persuasion, and technical writing.

Indicator 1. differentiate between stated and inferred main ideas and supporting details.

Indicator 2. differentiate between fact and opinion in a passage of text.

Indicator 3. identify author's point of view or bias.

Indicator 4. analyze the text for such structures as cause and effect, comparison and contrast, sequence, description, problem and solution, and narration, to aid in comprehension.

Indicator 5. evaluate the effectiveness of the text for the chosen purpose.

Indicator 6. summarize the text.

Indicator 7. synthesize important ideas from multiple sources.

Indicator 8. use a wide range of automatic monitoring and self-correction strategies to understand text.

Indicator 9. evaluate the clarity and accuracy of expository texts.

Standard 2: Learners write effectively for a variety of audiences, purposes, and contexts.

Benchmark 3: The proficient writer uses organization that enhances the reader's understanding.

Indicator 1. write introductions that draw the reader in and conclusions that leave the reader with a sense of resolution.

Indicator 2. use sequencing that is logical and effective.

Indicator 3. apply transitions clearly showing how ideas connect.

Indicator 4. use a variety of supporting details.

Indicator 5. organize so that the writing presentation flows smoothly.

Speaking, Viewing, Listening, Secondary

Standard 3: Learners will speak effectively for a variety of audiences, purposes, occasions, and con
texts.

Benchmark 3: The effective speaker produces a coherent message.

Indicator 1. use content consistent with the topic or purpose.

Indicator 2. use or create a product with sufficient detail for the topic.

Benchmark 5: The effective speaker demonstrates control of delivery skills.

Indicator 1. use an extemporaneous manner of delivery that creates speaker connection to audience.

Indicator 2. maintain an acceptable level of poise including eye contact, body position/
movement, and vocal expression (volume, pace, and inflection).

Indicator 3. use appropriate pronunciation and clear articulation.

Indicator 4. avoid distracting delivery behaviors such as fidgeting, rocking podium, shuffling notes,
and unintended verbal pauses.

Indicator 5. effectively use AV materials and equipment, such as charts, graphs, markerboards,
microphones, videos, overheads, and computer technology.

Information Power Information Literacy Standards and Indicators: 1.1, 1.4, 1.5, 2.1, 2.2, 2.3, 2.4, 3.1, 3.2, 3.3, 3.4,
5.3, 8.1, 8.2, 8.3, 9.1, 9.3, 9.4

Cooperative Teaching Plan:

Librarian Will:

■ Review with the teacher the appropriate historical victims of assassination based on available
materials and objectives of the unit.

■ Review the card catalog, magazine databases, proper Internet searching and use.

■ Brainstorm with students the most appropriate materials for the project.

■ Help students with note taking and citation skills.

■ Demonstrate use of *PowerPoint*.

■ Assist students who need help with design or technical difficulties on the computer.

■ Develop rubrics with the teacher to assess the project.

Teacher Will:

■ Review with the librarian the appropriate historical victims of assassination based on available
materials and objectives of the unit.

■ Assign students to work groups.

■ Assign assassination victim topics to the groups.

■ Guide students in reading for details and building on note taking skills.

■ Teach storyboarding and oral skills.

■ Help students use notes to develop well-constructed computer presentations.

■ Develop rubrics with the librarian to assess the project.

■ Assess the project based on the rubrics.

Resources:

Print

Assassinations. True Crime series. Richmond, Virginia: Time-Life Books, 1994.
Crimes and Punishment, 8 volume set. Marshall Cavendish, 1985.
Dictionary of American Biography. New York: Charles Schribners Sons, 1994.
Encyclopedia of World Biography. New York: Gale, 1998.
Great Events: The Twentieth Century. Englewood Cliffs, NJ: Salem Press, 1996.
Sifakis, Carl. *Encyclopedia of Assassinations.* New York: Facts on File, 1991.

Electronic

Online Databases (requires subscription):
    Infotrac. Gale Group.
    ProQuest, Resource/One. UMI
    SIRS Researcher. SIRS Mandarin, Inc.
"Assassinations and attempts in U.S. Since 1865." *Infoplease Almanac.* 24 July 2002
    <http://www.infoplease.com/ipa/A0194022.html>.
"On the Causes of War: 21 Political Assassinations Relevant to War", *Ground Zero Minnesota.*
    25 July 2002 <http://www.gzmn.org/v0000018.htm>.
"Political Assassinations." *Newsweek Archive.* 24 July 2002
    <http://archives.newsbank.com/newsweek>. (requires subscription for full text article)
"Political Assassinations." *Time Magazine Archive.* 24 July 2002
    <http://www.time.com/time/magazine/archive/>.

Audio Visual

Class of the 20th Century: Scrapbook of the Century. New York: A & E, 1996.
The Fabulous 60's. New York: MPI Home Video, 1985.
Great Events: The Twentieth Century. Englewood Cliffs, NJ: Salem Press, 1996.
History of the 20th Century. (10 volumes). New York: ABC Video Enterprises, Inc. 1980.

Equipment

PowerPoint software
Computers
Scanner
Video Projector or LCD panel

Product or Culminating Activity: A *PowerPoint* presentation to the class with at least six slides must address the who, what, where, when, why, and how of the victim's assassination, and finally, the effect the assassination had on history. This ties the project together with information skills and critical thinking skills, thus, it becomes a starting point for discussion on the importance of reading *Julius Caesar*.

Assessment Overview: The final presentation and a notetaking worksheet, citation worksheet, storyboard, and script are assessed primarily by the teacher, using the rubric developed by the teacher and the librarian. Emphasis is on the presentation and preparation of the assignment.

Adaptations and Extensions: This unit can be adapted for all students by assigning victims who are easier or more difficult to research. Deficits in computer skills can be compensated for by the choice of partners.

Notetaking Worksheet

Student Name: _____

RESEARCH ACTIVITY—VICTIMS OF ASSASSINATION

WHAT? _____
Person assassinated

WHEN? _____
Date of assassination

WHO? _____
Name/identification of assassins

WHERE? _____
Place of assassination

HOW? {Details of the assassination itself}

WHY? {Cause(s) Motive(s)}

BACKGROUND OF VICTIM {His/her importance, country, position}

EFFECTS {On others, on history, consequences of victim's death}

Sources Worksheet

Student Name_____

Assassination Victim: (Assigned by the teacher)_____
Date of Assassination: (Filled out by the teacher)_____

Locate several sources of information about your victim's assassination. For recent assassinations, *Reader's Guide* and some CD-ROMS will help you locate material in magazines. In the reference section, check the *Dictionary of American Biography, Encyclopedia of World Biography* and *Encyclopedia of Assassinations*.

List the sources you locate.

Books:

Author	Title	City	Publisher	Date
_____	_____	_____	_____	_____
_____	_____	_____	_____	_____

Magazines:

Author	Article Title	Magazine Title	Date	Page Number
_____	_____	_____	_____	_____
_____	_____	_____	_____	_____

Internet Citations:

Author	Title of Page	Title of Site	URL	Date
_____	_____	_____	_____	_____
_____	_____	_____	_____	_____

Other Sources:

Author	Title	Publisher	Date	Type of Media
_____	_____	_____	_____	_____
_____	_____	_____	_____	_____

Possible Assassination Victims

Cicero (43 B.C.)

Becket, Thomas (1170)

James I, King of Scotland (1437)

Lincoln, Abraham (April 14, 1865)

Garfield, James (July 2, 1881—Died Sept 19)

Evers, Medgar (June 12, 1963)

Archduke Ferdinand (June 28, 1914)

Moro, Aldo (May 9, 1978)

Rasputin (December 31, 1916)

Palme, Ololf (February 18, 1986)

Luxemburg, Rosa (January 15, 1919)

Zapata, Emiliano (April 10, 1919)

Villa, Pancho (June 20, 1923)

Kirov, Sergei (December 1, 1934)

Long, Huey (1935)

Trotsky, Leon (August 20, 1940)

Gandhi, Mohandas (January 30, 1948)

Trujillo, Rafael (May 30, 1961)

Kennedy, John F. (November 22, 1963)

Malcolm X or Malcolm Little (February 21, 1965)

Verwoerd, Henrik (September, 1966)

King, Martin Luther Jr. (April 4, 1968)

Kennedy, Robert F. (June 5, 1968)

King Faisal of Saudi Arabia (March 1975)

Chun Hee, Chun Hee (October 26, 1979)

Sadat, Anwar (October 1981)

Lennon, John (December 8, 1980)

Gemayel, Bashir (September 14, 1982)

Aquino, Benigno (August 21, 1983)

Gandhi, Indiria (October 31, 1984)

Wazir, Khalil (April 16, 1988)

Guevara, Ernesto "Che" (1967)

Rabin, Yitzhak (November, 1995)

Preparation Rubric

Locating Sources (20 Points)

Excellent	Satisfactory	Unsatisfactory	Evaluation
Demonstrates library skills to locate material independently in time allowed. Locates more than required number of sources from a variety of references. All citation information noted. 15–20 points	Demonstrates some library skills, but may not finish in time allowed. Locates required number of sources but some types of references not explored. Most citation information noted. 10–14 points	Demonstrates minimal library skills. Makes little progress in time allowed. Locates fewer than required number of sources from only one or two types of references. Little or no citation information noted. 0–9 points	

Note taking/Script (20 Points)

Excellent	Satisfactory	Unsatisfactory	Evaluation
Includes all relevant facts. Clear, easily understood. Written in own words. 15–20 points	Includes most relevant facts. Vague, meaning sometimes uncertain. Mostly in own words, some copied. 10–14 points	Incomplete facts. Difficult to understand. Copied. 0–9 points	

Storyboard/Documentation (20 Points)

Excellent	Satisfactory	Unsatisfactory	Evaluation
Accurate & meets all requirements. Logical organization. Effect on history is clear. Documentation always correct. 15–20 points	Accurate but only partial requirements met. Acceptable organization. Effect on history vague. Documentation mostly correct. 10–14 points	Inaccurate and/or incomplete Weak organization. History effect omitted. Documentation incorrect. 0–9 points	

Presentation Rubric

Speaking Skills (10 Points)

Excellent	Satisfactory	Unsatisfactory	Evaluation
Good eye contact; refers to notes sparingly. Speaks loudly, slowly and distinctly. Shows expression in voice. Very few distracting mannerisms.	Limited eye contact. Some material read from notes. Must be asked to speak up or repeat. Matter-of-fact tone of voice. Some minor distracting mannerisms.	Little or no eye contact. Speaks softly, mumbles. Voice sounds monotonous. Obvious distracting mannerisms.	
8–10 points	6–7 points	0–5 points	

PowerPoint Slides (20 Points)

Excellent	Satisfactory	Unsatisfactory	Evaluation
All computer functions* carried out independently. Font style and size, lines of text are easy to read and follow. Information presented in interesting and creative manner. Graphics clarify topic. Free of text errors.	Most computer functions* carried out with some help. Font style and size, lines of text require some explanation to read and follow. Information neat and interesting; shows evidence of planning. Graphics require explanation. Minor text errors.	Computer functions* completed with frequent help. Font size, lines of text are difficult to read and follow. Information poorly arranged; shows little planning. Graphics distract from topic. More than two errors.	
15–20 points	10–14 points	0–9 points	

Collaboration of Team (10 Points)

Excellent	Satisfactory	Unsatisfactory	Evaluation
Both team members share equally in process. Both share speaking responsibilities.	One member does most of preparatory work. One member does most of the speaking.	One member does little or no preparatory work or speaking.	
8–10 points	6–7 points	0–5 points	

*Computer functions: slide construction, inserting clip art, scan pictures, slide transitions, etc.

Recreating the American Civil War Era

Leslie Preddy, Library Media Specialist

Jenny Moore, Social Studies; Stephanie Quinlan, Mathematics; and

Howard Ely, Science Teacher

Perry Meridian Middle School

202 West Meridian School Road, Indianapolis, Indiana 46217

317-789-4100

lpreddy@msdpt.k12.in.uss

Grade Level: 8

Unit Overview: The goal of Recreating the American Civil War Era, a multidisciplinary unit, is to encourage eighth grade students to examine and collaboratively research the American Civil War. Research sources include the Internet as well as reference and non-fiction books, biographies, maps, and primary sources. Independently and in groups, students assemble projects, which may include artwork, collages, living stages, music, *PowerPoint* presentations, static displays, dioramas, and video productions. Students turn in a responsibility contract, source notes, bibliography, floor plan/storyboard, and research journal along with the final product. Their interactive displays become the backbone of *Civil War Day*, a Saturday community event.

Time Frame: 5 weeks

Content Area Standards: Indiana Academic Standards <http://www.doe.state.in.us/standards/welcome.html>
Correlation of the National Information Literacy Standards and the Indiana Academic Standards:
<http://www.doe.state.in.us/standards/ILS_Correlations.html>

English/Language Arts, Grade 8
8.4   Writing: Writing Process
8.41   Discuss ideas for writing, keep a list or notebook of ideas, and use graphic organizers to plan writing.
8.4.4   Plan and conduct multiple-step information searches by using computer networks.
8.4.5   Achieve an effective balance between researched information and original ideas.
8.4.8   Edit and proofread one's own writing, as well as that of others, using an editing checklist or set of rules, with specific examples of corrections of frequent errors.

8.5   Writing: Writing Applications (Different Types of Writing & Their Characteristics)
8.5.6   Write using precise word choices to make writing interesting and exact.

8.6   Writing: Written English Language Conventions
8.6.1   Use correct and varied sentence types (simple, compound, complex, and compound-complex) and sentence opening to present a lively and effective personal style.
8.6.5   Use correct punctuation.
8.6.6   Use correct capitalization.
8.6.7   Use correct spelling conventions.

8.7   Listening & Speaking: Listening & Speaking Skills, Strategies, & Applications

8.7.2   Match the message, vocabulary, voice modulation (change in tone), expression, and tone to the audience and purpose.

8.7.5   Use appropriate grammar, word choice, enunciation (clear speech), and pace (timing) during formal presentations.

8.7.6   Use audience feedback, including both verbal and nonverbal cues, to reconsider and modify the organization structure and/or to rearrange words and sentences for clarification of meaning.

8.7.12 Deliver a research presentation that:
- defines a thesis (a position on the topic).
- researches important ideas, concepts, and direct quotations from significant information sources and paraphrase and summarize important perspectives on the topic.
- uses a variety of research sources and distinguish the nature and value of each.
- presents information on charts, maps, and graphs.

Mathematics, Grade 8
8.1   Number Sense
8.12   Know that every rational number is either a terminating or repeating decimal and that every irrational number is a non-repeating decimal.

8.2   Computation
8.2.1   Add, subtract, multiply, and divide rational numbers (integers, fractions, and terminating decimals) in multi-step problems.

8.6   Data Analysis and Probability
8.6.1   Identify claims based on statistical data and, in simple cases, evaluate the reasonableness of the claims. Design a study to investigate the claim.

8.6.2   Identify different methods of selecting samples, analyzing the strengths and weaknesses of each method, and the possible bias in a sample or display.

8.6.4   Analyze, interpret, and display single- and two-variable data in appropriate bar, line and circle graphs, stem-and-leaf plots and box-and-whisker plots, and explain which types of display are appropriate for various data sets.

8.7   Problem Solving
8.7.4   Apply strategies and results from simpler problems to more complex problems.

8.7.6   Express the solution clearly and logically by using the appropriate mathematical terms and notations. Support solutions with evidence in both verbal and symbolic work.

8.7.7   Recognize the relative advantages of exact and approximate solutions to problems and give answers to a specified degree of accuracy.

8.7.10 Make precise calculations and check the validity of the results in the context of the problem

8.7.11 Decide whether a solution is reasonable in the context of the original situation.

Social Studies, Grade 8
8.1   Historical Knowledge
8.1.21 Analyze the causes and effects of events leading to the Civil War, including development of sectional conflict over slavery.

8.1.22 Describe the importance of key events in the Civil War, including the battles of Antietam, Vicksburg, and Gettysburg, and the Emancipation Proclamation and Gettysburg Address (1861–1865).

8.1.23 Explain and evaluate the policies, practices, and consequences of Reconstruction, including the Thirteenth, Fourteenth, and Fifteenth Amendments to the Constitution.

8.1.24 Identify the influence of individuals on political and social events and movements.

8.1.27 Recognize historical perspective by identifying the historical context in which events unfolded and by avoiding evaluation of the past solely in terms of present-day norms.

8.1.28 Identify, evaluate, and distinguish fact from opinion in a variety of information resources; differentiate between historical facts and interpretations, recognizing that the facts the historian reports reflect his or her judgment of what is most significant about the past.

8.1.29 Distinguish in historical narratives between unsupported expressions of opinion and informed hypothesis grounded in historical evidence.

8.1.30 Form historical research questions and seek responses by analyzing primary resources, such as autobiographies, diaries, maps, photographs, letters, and government documents and secondary resources, such as biographies and other non-fiction books and articles in the history of the United States.

8.3 Geography

8.3.6 Map changes in national boundaries, distribution of population, and economic activities at critical stages in development in the 18th and 19th centuries in the United States.

8.4 Economics

8.4.6 Analyze contributions of entrepreneurs, inventors, and other key individuals in the development of the United States economy.

8.4.7 Relate technological change and inventions to changes in labor productivity in the United States in the 18th and 19th centuries.

8.5 Individuals, Society, & Culture

8.5.6 Give examples of the changing role of women in the northern, southern, and western parts of the United States in the mid-19th century, and examine possible causes for these changes.

8.5.7 Give examples of scientific and technological developments that changed cultural life in the 19th-century United States…

8.5.8 Identify individuals in the arts and literature and their roles in portraying American culture in the nineteenth century…

8.5.9 Describe changes in entertainment and recreation, such as the growing interest in sports of various kinds in the mid-19th century, and explain how these changes related to urbanization and technological development.

8.5.10 Use a variety of information resources to identify examples of traditional arts, fine arts, music, and literature that reflect the ideals of American democracy in different historical periods, and plan presentation on or performances of selected works.

Information Power Information Literacy Standards and Indicators: 1.1, 1.2, 1.3, 1.4, 1.5, 2.1, 2.2, 2.3, 2.4, 3.1, 3.2, 3.3, 3.4, 5.3, 6.1, 6.2, 7.1, 8.3, 9.1, 9.2, 9.3, 9.4

Cooperative Teaching Plan:

Library Media Specialist Will:
- Notify the public library and coordinate the use of supplemental public library resources.
- Contact organizations in the Community Resources Packet: update information and notify those organizations of upcoming project and possible visitation from students.

- Prepare Instructional Media Center (IMC) resources for Medical Scavenger Hunt and Civil War research.
- Prepare and conduct mini-lessons based on the inquiry method: research topic selection, developing researchable questions, skimming for information, basic research methods, selecting an appropriate source, note taking, and citation.
- Arrange visits by students to present projects to area elementary school students.
- Organize and implement the student project competition for the *Civil War Day*.

Mathematics Teacher Will:

- Introduce the use and principles of proportion, data analysis, and sample versus population to analyze soldier casualties during each major battle of the Civil War in preparation for the "Ribbons" project.
- Issue each student either a blue or gray ribbon, which will represent a percentage of Union or Confederate soldiers. These ribbons will symbolically illustrate the effects of missing and imprisoned, dead, diseased, and wounded soldiers on the military population.
- Complete the "Ribbons" project during a statistical simulation with students on a life-size historical map of the United States.

Social Studies Teacher Will:

- Provide students with an overview of the social and historical issues of the Civil War.
- Collaborate with the library media specialist to develop, implement, evaluate, and revise an inquiry research project that includes the following:
  - Students will be given choices of topics to collaboratively research.
  - Students will turn in a written proposal, daily reflections, source notes, bibliography, floor plan/story board, and research journal.
  - Students assemble their projects, which may include a living stage, static display, art, PowerPoint, collage, and/or music.
  - Exhibition of the projects consists of oral and physical presentations.
  - Students prepare these displays for area elementary schools and *Civil War Day*.

Science Teacher Will:

- Provide students with an overview of scientific innovations during the Civil War period.
- Partner with the library media specialist to develop and implement a scavenger hunt for students to research the influence and impact of technology in the areas of medicine and disease. The Medical Scavenger Hunt allows students to study disease and changes in treatment from the Civil War to today.

Teachers and Library Media Specialist Will Jointly:

- Host a Parent Information Night: share with parents student expectations, timeline, and resources (people, Web sites, museums, institutions) available.
- Attend and participate in weekly meetings to plan, host, and run the *Civil War Day*.
- Assist students individually and in small groups with research challenges.
- Host after-school help sessions in the Instructional Media Center.
- Team IMC use so that students have two periods per day to research when in the IMC.
- Coordinate with the PTA for volunteers to help during the *Civil War Day*.
- Organize publicity and re-enactors for the *Civil War Day*.
- Observe and grade students' research process, final project, and presentation.
- Post-assess the multidisciplinary unit and *Civil War Day* for revision for next year.

Resources:

Print

Arms and Equipment of the Union and *Arms and Equipment of the Confederacy*. Alexandria, Virginia: Time-Life Books, 1998.

Axelrod, Alan. *Complete Idiot's Guide to the Civil War.* New York: Alpha Books, 1998.

Baker, Lawrence W., ed. *American Civil War: A Multicultural Encyclopedia*, 7 volumes. Danbury, Connecticut: Grolier, 1994.

Bradford, Ned, ed. *Battle and Leaders of the Civil War*. 4 vols. New York: Thomas Yoseloff, 1956.

The Confederacy. New York: Simon & Schuster, 1993.

Cornerstones of Freedom series. New York: Children's Press.

Erdosh, George. *Food and Recipes of the Civil War (Cooking Throughout American History* series). New York: Rosen Publishing Group, 1997.

Kalman, Bobbie. *19th Century Clothing (Historic Communities* series). Toronto: Crabtree, 1993.

Savage, Douglas J. *Untold History of the Civil War* series. Philadelphia: Chelsea House.

UXL American Civil War Reference Library, 5 volumes. Detroit: UXL, 2000.

Watts, J. F. and Fred L. Israel, eds. *Presidential Documents*. New York: Routledge, 2000.

Electronic

"Camp Life: Civil War Collections from Gettysburg National Military Park." *National Park Service.* 25 July 2002
<http://www.cr.nps.gov/museum/exhibits/gettex/index.htm>.

"Civil War Battle Summaries by State/Campaign." *National Park Service.* 24 July 2002
<http://www2.cr.nps.gov/abpp/battles/bystate.htm>.

"Civil War Maps." *American Memory: Library of Congress.* 15 December 1999. 24 July 2002
<http://memory.loc.gov/ammem/gmdhtml/cwmhtml/cwmhome.html>

"Civil War Soldiers and Sailors System." *National Park Service.* 24 July 2002
<http://www.itd.nps.gov/cwss/index.html>.

"A Nation Divided: The U.S. Civil War 1861-1865." *The History Place™.* 24 July 2002
<http://www.historyplace.com/civilwar/index.html>.

"Selected Civil War Photographs." *Library of Congress.* 15 January 2000. 11 24 July 2002
<http://memory.loc.gov/ammem/cwphtml/cwphome.html>.

"Symbols in Battle: Civil War Flags in NPS Collections." *National Park Service*, 7 December 1999. 24 July 2002 <http://www.cr.nps.gov/csd/exhibits/flags/>.

"Valley of the Shadow: Two Communities in the American Civil War." *The Institute for Advanced Technology in the Humanities, University of Virginia.* 24 July 2002
<http://jefferson.village.virginia.edu/vshadow2/>.

Audiovisual

Glory. Videocassette. Tri-Star Pictures, 1989.

Harper's Weekly: Journal of Civilization. CD-ROM. Bedford, Massachusetts: Applewood Books, 2000.

Other

A favorite resource is Scrapbook/Memory Books of trips the students' classroom teachers and library media specialist have taken to sites of historical significance to the American Civil War. These books include photographs, maps, flyers, postcards, and research and interview notes educators have compiled.

Product or Culminating Activity: The culmination of the five-week unit is the community event—*Civil War Day*—in which the community and neighboring schools are invited to participate in a day of education and fun. Students and professional re-enactors work beside each other to present their knowledge to the attending community. We turn our students into teachers as they present their projects in a variety of ways that help to reinforce what has been learned. Our students' experiences enhance their learning as they step into the role of teacher.

Assessment Overview: Students are evaluated in three ways:

1. Students are given a timeline with mini-deadlines within the big project. Meeting each mini-deadline earns credit. Smaller deadlines within the large project aid students in handling the unit in manageable steps and keep them on-task.
2. Students receive a grade for the research process. Did he/she stay on task? Did he/she accept a setback as a challenge and continue to strive to find the information? Did he/she ask for help when needed? Did he/she heed the guidance and research advice given? Did the student learn?
3. Students are also given a grade on the final project and oral presentation of that project. It is possible for a student to receive an excellent grade for the research process and a mediocre grade for the final project and presentation.

| Figure 4.73 | Recreating the American Civil War Era |

Assignment Description

Name _____   Date _____

- You will choose a topic and conduct detailed investigative research.
- You will create a visual and oral product with the new knowledge you have gained.
  - Your presentations must be well done, colorful, creative, and detailed.
  - Your oral presentation will last a minimum of 10 minutes.
- This project may be completed as an individual or group with the understanding that group grades will involve a point split—half of the grade will be a group grade and half an individual grade. Therefore, if a group member does not work, he/she will receive the same group grade, but will not receive the same individual grade. Choose your partners wisely!

As the projects advance you will complete several steps along the way. Each group or individual is responsible for meeting deadlines. If a group member is absent on the day something is due, other group members must turn it in. Remember, groups put in a group effort! Keep all papers related to your project in your research journal. Stay updated on the progress of your group and your own progress every day. Meet all deadlines and due dates!

Meeting Deadlines

- The point breakdown of this project is available on your Rubric Grade Chart.
- Be sure to take a look at each step of the project, due dates, and point values along the way. Any questions need to be addressed immediately.
- In Social Studies class, this is worth 400 points—half of your six week grade—so be responsible.
- Good luck and have a great time!

Final Project Presentation Options

- You must choose at least two presentation options in order to receive a full grade.
- A time will be assigned to you if you do not sign up.
- Be sure to follow the rules of signing up and honor your presentation time.
- Attend both of your presentations. No unexcused absence or missed presentation is allowed.
  - Make-up time and date for a missed presentation is at the teacher's discretion.
  - Individual members of groups who do not show up for presentation times will be given an automatic zero for that presentation and removed from the group.
  - A doctor's note is the only accepted excuse for missing a presentation time.

Sign up for TWO of the presentation options:
Option #1 – After school (May chose only one)
Option #2 – During class only (May chose only one)
Option #3 – Elementary school (May choose only one) **After-school audition required**
Option #4 – Civil Way Day Celebration 2001 (Saturday)

Figure 4.74 **Recreating the American Civil War Era**

Civil War Medical Term Scavenger Hunt

Terms	Definition	Treatment (THEN)	Treatment (NOW)
1. Antibiotics			
2. Diarrhea			
3. Dysentery			
4. Immunity			
5. Measles			
6. Mumps			
7. Pneumonia			
8. Tetanus			
9. Typhoid Fever			
10. Typhus			
11. Vaccine			
12. Morphine			
13. Laudanum			
14. Ether			
15. Amputation			
16. Chloroform			
17. Small Pox			
18. Gangrene			
19. Scurvy			
20. Malaria			

Figure 4.75   Recreating the American Civil War Era

Unit Plan Organizer

Project Title: Ribbons
Subject Area: Mathematics

Objectives: Students will analyze statistics concerning the casualties of the Civil War to better understand the devastation it caused. Using the concept of sample versus population, each student will wear a ribbon representing a percentage of soldiers who fought and were afflicted/casualties during the Civil War. After each significant battle, the students will tally the casualties (deaths, MIA/POWs, wounded, diseased) and use proportions to determine how many students will be *afflicted* with each calamity. Colored stickers will represent each of the casualties and will be placed on the appropriate ribbons. A simple roll of the dice will decide which students to afflict (one roll for class period, one roll for student row, and one roll for the seat within the row) with each of the predetermined casualties. Everything will be done at the beginning of a class period, for 10-15 minutes. No significant changes of the school's curriculum or subject time line will be affected.

Unit Plan Summary:

Day 1:
1. Explain the goals and objectives of the Ribbon project.
2. Explain sample vs. population. Example: Nielson ratings for TV.
3. After receiving the total casualties (1,560,000) and using proportions, students determine the number of soldiers each ribbon represents (approximately 10,400 for a team/class of 150 students).
4. Issue ribbons to each student. Students do the math being certain that 72% of students in each class are blue and 28% are gray (representing the Union and the Confederacy).
5. Students must bring ribbons to class and participate in the calculations and discussions everyday to receive their points for this project.

Days 2-13:
1. Place the battle studied today in Social Studies class and the battle's casualties in a chart on the board for students to copy in their math journals. (Numbers are close estimates.)
2. In their journals, students calculate totals and determine how many ribbons will receive stickers today (White= MIA/POW, Red=Wounded, Yellow=Diseased, Black=Dead). Any total below one sample soldier, or ribbon (10,400), will be rounded up to one. All others will use the math rule for rounding to a whole number.
3. In homeroom, roll dice to determine which class periods will have the afflicted soldiers.
4. Roll dice to determine the row and seat of each of the afflicted soldiers. Dispense stickers.

* A discussion on probability is added to this unit on a daily basis

Figure 4.75   **(continued from page 195)**

Day 14:

> Based on what they have seen during the Ribbons project, students will estimate
> the percentage of students in their class who are:
> 1. Dead
> 2. Missing or taken prisoner
> 3. Wounded
> 4. Diseased
> 5. Had no casualties/injury
> 6. Had more than one casualty/injury

Day 15:

> Using totals from the entire team/class, students will calculate the percentage of students in their
> class who are:
> 1. Dead
> 2. Missing or taken prisoner
> 3. Wounded
> 4. Diseased
> 5. Had no casualties/injury
> 6. Had more than one casualty/injury
>
> Compare yesterday's estimate to the actual percentages.
> Compare each class to the whole team's percentages.
> Students will be expected to wear their ribbons for the entire last day of the Ribbons project.

Day 16:

> Discuss the devastating effect the war had on the soldiers. Students will have had the day to walk
> through the school seeing their classmates' ribbons and the small number of students without any
> casualties.

Day 17:

> Take the team of students (150 students) to the life-size map for the statistical simulation.

Materials Used:

> 1. Custom-made Ellison die-cut press ribbons (one CSA and one USA)
> 2. Construction paper (gray and blue)
> 3. Round colored coding labels (white, red, black, and yellow)
> 4. Safety pins
> 5. Overhead dice

Resources:

Bradford, Ned, ed. *Battle and Leaders of the Civil War*. 4 vols. New York: Thomas Yoseloff, 1956.

| Figure 4.76 | Recreating the American Civil War Era |

Sample Math Lesson Plan Organizer

Project Title: Ribbons
Subject Area: Mathematics
Teacher name:
Lesson: 4/Battle at Shiloh

Objectives: Students will see the number of casualties during the battle at Shiloh.
Students will use sample vs. population to calculate and determine the number of students in their class who will represent the casualties.

Lesson: Teacher puts the following chart on the board:

	Wounded	Dead	MIA/POW	Diseased
Union	8,012	1,723	959	36,263
Confederacy	8,408	1,754	2,885	33,478
Total				
Stickers				

Remember: 1 sticker = 10,400 stickers

Each student should copy and complete the table in his/her journal, calculate the total casualties for this battle, and determine the number of students (rounding to the nearest whole number) to represent the afflicted soldiers. The completed table would look like this:

	Wounded	Dead	MIA/POW	Diseased
Union	8,012	1,723	959	36,263
Confederacy	8,408	1,754	2,885	33,478
Total	16,420	3,477	3,844	69,741
Students	2	1	1	7

In homeroom, teacher rolls the dice to determine from which class period the *afflicted* soldiers will come. Then he/she rolls the dice in each class period to find the exact student who will be *afflicted* and given a round color-coded sticker (representing that affliction) to place on his/her ribbon (one roll for the student row and one roll for the student seat).

Continue with the regular math lesson...

Figure 4.77   **Recreating the American Civil War Era**

Community Resources Packet

The library media specialist will update the Packet created for parents and students and will:
- ■ confirm contact name, street address, phone, email, Internet address and make corrections;
- ■ update as necessary the hours of operation, fees, and other operational details;
- ■ include an annotation of the organization's procedures, policies, and resources available to the public that relate to the American Civil War.

The three sections of the Community Resources Packet include the following organizations:

COMMUNITY RESOURCES
Indiana Historical Society
Indiana State Archives
Indiana State Library-
   Indiana Division
Indiana State Museum
IUPUI University Library
Indianapolis-Marion
   County Public Library

HISTORIC SITES & MUSEUMS
Arsenal Technical High School
Camp Morton
Colonel Eli Lilly Civil War Museum
Corydon & Battle of Corydon
Memorial Park
Crown Hill Cemetery
Hannah House Museum
Indiana War Memorial –
   Battle Flag Collection
Levi Coffin House Museum
Military Park

INTERNET RESOURCES
Harper's Weekly Online
Library of Congress
U.S. Army Center of Military
   History
National Park Service
Smithsonian-National
   Museum of American
   History

SAMPLE ENTRY
Indiana State Archives

Indiana State Archives
(near Arlington & Shadeland)
6440 East 30th
Indianapolis, IN 46219
phone 591-5220
http://www.state.in.us/icpr/webfile/archives/homepage.html

Hours:
Monday-Friday 8:00-4:30

Extensive collection for Indiana Civil War Regiments and individual soldiers. Contains Civil War mustering records with physical descriptions, when mustered in, and when left and why. It also holds regimental correspondence, clothing books, hospital records, rosters, draft enrollments, ordinance records, etc. Some of the standard reference tools they have can give you information as specific as the average height of a soldier, etc.

Sign in at the registration desk and ask for help finding the information you need. Make sure you arrive with a specific project in mind and ideas about what information you need.

Figure 4.78 **Recreating the American Civil War Era**

Judges' Guidelines

10:40	Judges' meeting in the main office
10:55	Judges quickly peruse all projects in the IMC
11:00	Judging begins
12:00	Judging ends & contestants dismissed
12:05	Complete judging forms tallied in tally room
1:15	PA announcement for all contestants to report to IMC
1:30	8 Semi-Finalists announced and semi-finalists re-judged
2:00	4 Place winners announced

- Only evaluate the project stationed within the highlighted area on your map.
- Due to time restrictions, you will only be given five minutes with each project.
- Each project has been given an ID number. Please place that number in the box on the judging form before you begin your evaluation.
- Engage the students in conversation—allow them the opportunity to share their expertise with you. Try to elicit verbal response from all team members.
- Give the students an opportunity to explain their visuals to you.
- Be honest in your scoring!
- Do not show completed forms to students.
- At the end of judging, please turn your completed form in for tallying.

Figure 4.79 **Recreating the American Civil War Era**

Judging Form for Civil War Day Celebration

Judges: Please complete for each project you evaluate.
Be sure to fill in a score for each category.
Ask students questions to better determine their score.
Please check the corresponding box to score each category.

Please do not total the score. That will be done in the tally room.
Good luck and have fun!

Project ID #

Category	Ratings			
	1- okay	2-good	3-excellent	4-perfect
1. Appearance: creative, colorful, organized, neatness				
2. Workmanship: interesting, plagiarism, etc.				
3. Historically accurate				
4. Presentation: students able to verbalize knowledge				
5. Students able to prove original work (minimal parent help)				

6. Is the project non-static (interactive)?	YES	NO	
7. Are all team members for the project present?	YES	NO	

Figure 4.80   **Recreating the American Civil War Era**

Responsibility Contract

Student Name _____   Date _____

My topic choice is _____

Things I want to learn during my research are _____

_____

_____

_____

_____

My project format choice is _____

My presentation time choices are: 1_____

                                     2_____

Full Names of Group Members, if working in a group, including yourself:

RESEARCH RUBRIC/GRADE CHART

- Complete each item by the deadline.
- Bring the completed item and your rubric to a teacher to receive a teacher's signature.
- A teacher's signature will be required in order to earn the points.
- Be sure to meet every deadline.
- This is the only record of your grade. If this sheet is lost you will lose the points you have accumulated to that point. You may have another sheet to continue with the project, but the prior points received on the lost sheet will be deducted from your grade.

Student's signature _____
I have read through my project requirements and due dates. I understand the penalties for not completing a requirement by the date due.

Parent signature _____
I have read my student's requirements and understand the consequences if he/she fails to complete the required tasks by the date due.

There will be no permanent record of your points except the following sheet.

Figure 4.81   **Recreating the American Civil War Era**

Research Rubric/Grade Chart

Teacher's Signature	Date Due	CONTENT	Points Possible	Points Earned
		SCIENCE		
		Inventor/Invention		
		Daily Effort*	30	
		Scavenger Hunt	100	
		SOCIAL STUDIES		
		Civil War Research		
		Daily Effort*	50	
		Daily Reflection Worksheet	20	
		Responsibility Contract	20	
		Source Note check	10	
		Presentation sign-up	10	
		Floor Plan/Storyboard	20	
		Source Note check	10	
		Bibliography rough draft	10	
		Research Notebook	30	
		Final Bibliography	20	
		Civil War Day – extra credit		
		attendance-extra credit	25	
		participation-extra credit	25	
		SCIENCE Content Points	**130**	
		S. S. Content Points	**200**	

Final Project Grades	Possible	Earned
Product		
historical accuracy	20	
research included / evident	20	
creative, color, organized, imaginative	20	
followed instructions / shows effort	20	
Presentation 1 on-time	10	
verbalization of knowledge	20	
interesting / enthusiastic	10	
reaches intended audience / eye contact/voice	10	
followed instructions / shows effort	10	
Presentation 2 on-time	10	
verbalization of knowledge	20	
interesting / enthusiastic	10	
reaches intended audience / eye contact/voice	10	
followed instructions / shows effort	10	
PROJECT POINTS	**200**	

*DAILY EFFORT: An instructional media center grade will be given daily based on preparation, effort, staying on-task, not distracting others, asking an expert for help when you need it, etc.

Top 10 Lists for the Millennium

Nan Sprester, Librarian
Sharon Hubbard, English Teacher
Brewer Middle School
1000A S. Cherry Lane, Ft. Worth, Texas 76108
817-367-1267
nasprester@kellerisd.net

Grade Level: 7 & 8

Unit Overview: Working in small groups, middle school students compile "Top 10 Lists for the Millennium." Each group selects a topic from the list provided and, through research and higher level thinking, ranks the 10 most important events/people/contributions within their topic from the last 1,000 years. Students present their lists to the class through either oral or visual presentations.

Time Frame: 4 weeks

Content Area Standards: Texas Essential Knowledge and Skills
<http://www.tea.state.tx.us/teks>

110.21. Implementation of Texas Essential Knowledge and Skills, English Language Arts and Reading, Middle School
110.23 English Language Arts and Reading, Grade 7
110.24 English Language Arts and Reading, Grade 8

6-8.8   Reading/variety of texts. The student reads widely for different purposes in varied sources.
8. D.   Read to take action such as to complete forms, make informed recommendations, and write a response (6-8)

6-8.10. Reading/comprehension. The student uses a variety of strategies to comprehend a wide range of texts of increasing levels of difficulty.
10. A.   Use his/her own knowledge and experience to comprehend (4-8)
10. B.   Establish and adjust purposes for reading such as reading to find out, to understand, to interpret, to enjoy, and to solve problems (4-8)
10. C.   Monitor his/her own comprehension and make modifications when understanding breaks down such as by rereading a portion aloud, using reference aids, searching for clues, and asking questions (4-8)
10. E.   Use the text's structure or progression of ideas such as cause and effect or chronology to locate and recall information (4-8)
10. G.   Paraphrase and summarize text to recall, inform, or organize ideas (4-8)
10. H.   Draw inferences such as conclusions or generalizations and support them with text evidence and experience (4-8)
10. I.   Find similarities and differences across texts such as in treatment, scope, or organization (4-8)
10. J.   Distinguish fact and opinion in various texts (4-8)
10. L.   Represent text information in different ways such as in outline, timeline, or graphic organizer (4-8)

6-8.11 Reading/literary response. The student expresses and supports responses to various types of texts.

11 A.   Offer observations, make connections, react, speculate, interpret, and raise questions in response to texts (4-8)

11 B.   Interpret text ideas through such varied means journal writing, discussion, enactment, and media (4-8)

11 D.   Connect, compare, and contrast ideas, themes, and issues across text (4-8)

6-8.13. Reading/inquiry/research. The student inquires and conducts research using a variety of sources.

13. A.   Form and revise questions for investigations, including questions arising from readings, assignments, and units of study (6-8)

13. B.   Use text organizers, including headings, graphic features, and tables of contents, to locate and organize information (4-8)

13. C.   Use multiple sources, including electronic texts, experts, and print resources, to locate information relevant to research questions (4-8)

13. D.   Interpret and use graphic sources of information such as maps, graphs, timelines or tables to address research questions (4-8)

13. E.   Summarize and organize information from multiple sources by taking notes, outlining ideas, and making charts (4-8)

13. F.   Produce research projects and reports in effective formats for various audiences (6-8)

13. G.   Draw conclusions from information gathered from multiple sources (4-8)

13. H.   Use compiled information and knowledge to raise additional, unanswered questions (3-8)

13. I.   Present organized statements, reports, and speeches using visuals or media to support meaning (6-8)

6-8.20. Writing/inquiry/research. The student uses writing as a tool for learning and research.

20. A.   Frame questions to direct research (4-8)

20. B.   Organize prior knowledge about a topic in a variety of ways such as by producing a graphic organizer (4-8)

20. C.   Take notes from relevant and authoritative sources such as guest speakers, periodicals, and on-line searches (4-8)

20. D.   Summarize and organize ideas gained from multiple sources in useful ways such as outlines, conceptual maps, learning logs, and timelines (4-8)

20. E.   Present information in various forms using available technology (4-8)

20. F.   Evaluate his/her own research and frame new questions for further investigation (4-8)

20. G.   Follow accepted formats for writing research, including documenting sources (6-8)

113.21 Implementation of Texas Essential Knowledge and Skills for Social Studies, Middle School
113.23 Social Studies, Grade 7
113.24 Social Studies, Grade 8

7.21, 8.30. Social studies skills. The student applies critical-thinking skills to organize and use information acquired from a variety of sources including electronic technology.

7.21. A. Differentiate between, locate, and use primary and secondary sources such as computer software, databases, media and news services, biographies, interviews, and artifacts to acquire information.

7.21. B. Analyze information by sequencing, categorizing, identifying cause-and-effect relationships, comparing, contrasting, finding the main idea, summarizing, making generalizations and predictions, and drawing inferences and conclusions.

7.21. C. Organize and interpret information from outlines, reports, databases, and visuals including graphs, charts, timelines, and maps.

7.21. D. Identify points of view from the historical context surrounding an event and the frame of reference that influenced the participants.

7.21. E. Support a point of view on a social studies issue or event.

7.21. F. Identify bias in written, oral, and visual material.

7.21. G. Evaluate the validity of a source based on language, corroboration with other sources, and information about the author.

7.22, 8.31 Social studies skills. The student communicates in written, oral, and visual forms.

7.22. B. Use standard grammar, spelling, sentence structure, and punctuation.

7.22. C. Transfer information from one medium to another, including written to visual and statistical to written or visual, using computer software as appropriate; and

7.22. D. Create written, oral, and visual presentations of social studies information.

7.23, 8.32. Social studies skills. The student uses problem-solving and decision-making skills, working independently and with others, in a variety of settings.

7.23. A. Use a problem-solving process to identify a problem, gather information, list and consider options, consider advantages and disadvantages, choose and implement a solution, and evaluate the effectiveness of the solution.

7.23. B. Use a decision-making process to identify a situation that requires a decision, gather information, identify options, predict consequences, and take action to implement a decision.

8.29. Science, technology, and society. The student understands the impact of scientific discoveries and technological innovations on daily life in the United States. The student is expected to:

8.29. A. Compare the effects of scientific discoveries and technological innovations that have influenced daily life in different periods in U.S. history.

8.29. B. Describe how scientific ideas influenced technological developments during different periods in U.S. history.

Information Power Information Literacy Standards and Indicators: 1.1, 1.2, 1.3, 1.4, 2.1, 2.2, 2.4, 3.1, 3.2, 3.3, 3.4, 5.2, 5.3, 9.1, 9.3, 9.4

Cooperative Teaching Plan:

Librarian Will:
- Introduce category choices and help the groups brainstorm topics and questions to consider in their research.
- Introduce the research process.
- Instruct students in location and use of reference materials, both print and electronic.
- Assist students with research.
- Instruct students on note taking.

Teacher Will:

- Introduce the unit.
- Facilitate cooperative learning groups.
- Assist in the planning of presentations.
- Evaluate presentations.

Resources:

Print

Adams, Laurie. *Art Across Time.* Boston: McGraw Hill College, 1999.

Art: A World History. New York: DK Publishers, 1998.

The Associated Press Library of Disasters. Danbury, Connecticut: Grolier Educational, 1997.

Bruno, Leonard C. *Science and Technology Breakthroughs: From the Wheel to the World Wide Web.* Detroit: UXL, 1998.

Chisholm, Jane. Usborne *Timelines of World History.* Tulsa, Oklahoma: Usborne, 2001.

Compton's Encyclopedia & Fact Index. Elmhurst, Illinois. Success Pub. Group, 2001.

Curl, James Stevens. *Dictionary of Architecture.* New York: Oxford University Press, 1999.

Curtis, Robert H. *Great Lives: Medicine.* New York: Atheneum, 1993.

Cyclopedia of World Authors. Pasadena, California: Salem Press, 1997.

The Dorling Kindersley History of the World. New York: Dorling Kindersley, 1994.

Encyclopedia of World Facts and Dates. New York: HarperCollins, 1993.

Encyclopedia of World History. New York: Facts On File, 2000.

Government Leaders, Military Rulers, and Political Activists: An Encyclopedia of People Who Changed the World. Westport, Connecticut: Oryx Press, 2001.

Harding, Anne S. *Milestones in Health and Medicine.* Phoenix: Oryx Press, 2000.

Herstory: Women Who Changed the World. New York: Viking, 1995.

Inventions and Inventors. Danbury, Connecticut: Grolier Educational, 2000.

Medical Discoveries: Medical Breakthroughs and the People Who Developed Them. Detroit: UXL, 1997.

Merriam-Webster's Biographical Dictionary. Springfield, Massachusetts: Merriam-Webster, 1995.

The Oxford Children's Book of Famous People. New York: Oxford University Press, 1999.

Paparchontis, Kathleen. *100 World Leaders Who Shaped World History.* San Mateo, California: Bluewood Books, 2001.

Reichold, Klaus. *Buildings That Changed the World.* New York: Prestel, 1999.

Rolka, Gail Meyer. *100 Women Who Shaped World History.* San Francisco: Bluewood Books, 1994.

Sachs, Jessica Snyder. *The Encyclopedia of Inventions.* New York: Franklin Watts, 2001.

Slonimsky, Nicolas. *The Great Composers and Their Works.* New York: Schirmer Books, 2000.

Stevenson, Neil. *Architecture.* New York: DK Publishers, 1997.

Streissguth, Thomas. *Communications: Sending the Message.* Minneapolis: Oliver Press, 1997.

Sutton, Ian. *Western Architecture: From Ancient Greece to the Present.* London: Thames & Hudson, 1999.

Wilkinson, Philip. *Transportation.* New York: Chelsea House Publishers, 1995.

Wilson, Anthony. *Dorling Kindersley Visual Timeline of Transportation.* New York: Dorling Kindersley, 1995.

World Book Encyclopedia. Chicago: World Book Inc., 2001.

World Leaders: People Who Shaped the World. Detroit: UXL 1994.

Electronic

Online Databases (requires subscription):

Biography Resource Center. Gale Group.

Info-Trac Jr. Edition. Gale Group.

Art History Network. 24 July 2002 <http://www.arthistory.net/>.

Biography.com. 24 July 2002 <http:www.biography.com>.

Cobblestone History-Social Science. CD-ROM. Peterborough, New Hampshire: Cobblestone Publishing 1998.

"The History of Invention." *CBC4Kids.* 24 July 2002 <http://www.cbc4kids.ca/general/the-lab/history-of-invention/default.html>.

Microsoft Encarta Encyclopedia 2000. CD-ROM. Redmond, Washington: Microsoft Corporation, 2000.

"World History." *InfoPlease.com.* 24 July 2002 <http://www.infoplease.com/ipa/A0001196.html>.

The World History Database. 24 July 2002 <http://www.worldhistory.com>.

Product or Culminating Activity: Student groups will present their Top 10 lists to the class through either a poster, timeline, children's book, videotape, teaching a lesson to the class, or a panel discussion.

Assessment Overview: Teacher assessment based on depth of research, criteria used for ranking, contribution to group, neatness, and accuracy.

Adaptations: Students could use their research to create a millennium museum and invite parents and community members to view it.

Each class could be limited to only one broad category, such as people, events, inventions, etc. Small groups would then be assigned narrower topics within the category. Then the groups would be rearranged to include one member from each of the first groups. Then these groups would be required to create a Top 10 list for the broader category based on their individual research.

| Figure 4.82 | Top 10 Lists for the Millennium |

Assignment Overview

ASSIGNMENT

Your group will create a list of the Top 10 most important events/people/contributions from the last 1,000 years within a selected topic. Your group will also make a presentation to the class. You may use any of the types of presentations listed below or you may select another type with approval of the instructor. Please fill your presentation with facts, illustrations, and demonstrations whenever possible. Be sure to explain why your group created the list you did. Try to identify any cause and effect relationships you discover in your research.

PRESENTATIONS

Teach a lesson to the class using handouts, transparencies, worksheets, etc.
*Poster(s)   *Timeline   *Panel discussion   *Children's Book   *Class lesson   *Videotape

GROUPS

Groups will consist of two to four members, who will be assigned by the teacher.

RESEARCH CATEGORIES

Inventions	Visual arts	Natural disasters
World leaders	Authors	Composers
Medical advances	Women	Architecture
Transportation	Communication	Explorers

PROCEDURE

1. Select a topic from the list.
   Assignment: Create a list of the top 10_____ of the millennium.
2. Develop who, what, when, where, how and why questions for your topic.
3. Find your topic in the encyclopedia. With your group, brainstorm and make a list of 20 possible items to include.
4. Each member of the group should select five items to research.
5. Generate keywords to use during Internet and OPAC searches.
6. Use reference books, Web sites, encyclopedia, magazines, etc., to answer the questions developed in Step 2. Use the note-taking grid for your research.
7. As a group, narrow your list to 10 and rank them.
8. Choose a project to present from the list and delegate responsibilities.
9. Self-evaluation: Ask these questions before making the presentation:
   Are your facts correct?
   Did you use complete sentences?
   Are your spelling and grammar correct?
   Is enough information included?

Figure 4.83 Top 10 Lists for the Millennium

Note-Taking Grid

Student Name	Question	Question
Topic	Key Words	Key Words

BOOK SOURCE
    Author
 	
      Title
 	
      Place of Publication
 	
      Publisher
 	
      Copyright Date
	Notes	Notes

INTERNET SOURCE
    Author (if given)
 	
      Title of Page
 	
      Web site
 	
      Date (if given)
 	
      Date Accessed
 	
      URL
	Notes	Notes

Figure 4.84 **Top 10 Lists for the Millennium**

Rubric for Poster, Timeline, Children's Book

CATEGORY	10	8	6	4
Neatness	Work is very neat and presentable.	Work is neat and presentable.	Work is somewhat neat.	Work is messy/ difficult to read.
Accuracy	All facts on the work are correct.	Fewer than 3 facts on the work are incorrect.	Fewer than 6 facts on the work are incorrect.	More than 6 facts on the work are incorrect.
Spelling	There are no misspelled words.	Fewer than 5 words words are misspelled.	Fewer than 10 words are misspelled.	More than 10 words are misspelled.
Punctuation	There are no punctuation errors.	There are fewer than 5 errors in punctuation.	There are fewer than 10 errors in punctuation.	There are more than 10 errors in punctuation
Grammar	There are no errors in grammar.	There are fewer than 5 errors in grammar.	There are fewer than 10 errors in grammar.	There are more than 10 errors in grammar.
Information Included	Thoroughly describes 10 items with several supporting facts about each.	Describes 10 items with many supporting facts about each.	Describes 10 items with a few supporting facts about each.	Lists 10 or fewer items with no supporting facts.
Knowledge Gained	Student can accurately answer all questions related to the work.	Student can accurately answer most questions related to the work.	Student can accurately answer some questions related to the work.	Student can answer no questions related to the work.
Reasoning	The reasons for the ranking of the top 10 are very logical.	The reasons for the ranking of the top 10 are logical.	The reasons for the ranking of the top 10 are not logical.	There are no reasons given to explain the ranking.
Graphics	Graphics are effective and complement the text.	Graphics are effective but there are too few or too many.	Some graphics are effective.	Graphics are not effective or are absent.
Preparation	The student has notes about all the events and dates included.	The student has notes about almost all the events and dates included.	The student has notes about a few of the events and dates included.	The student has no notes.

Figure 4.85 **Top 10 Lists for the Millennium**

Rubric for Oral Presentation

CATEGORY	10	8	6	4
Knowledge Gained	Student can accurately answer all questions.	Student can accurately answer most questions.	Student can accurately answer. some questions.	Student cannot answer questions related to the work.
Eye Contact	All presenters maintain good eye contact during the lesson.	Most presenters maintain good eye contact during the lesson.	Most presenters maintain some eye contact during the lesson.	Very little eye contact made.
Props	Many props or visual aids used.	Some props or visual aids used.	A few props or visual aids used.	No props or visual aids used.
Preparation	The student has notes about all events and dates included.	The student has notes about most events and dates included.	The student has notes about a few of the events and dates included.	The student has no notes.
Reasoning	The reasons for the ranking of the top 10 are exceptionally logical.	The reasons for the ranking of the top 10 are logical.	The reasons for the ranking of the top 10 are not logical.	There are no reasons given to explain the ranking.
Length of Presentation	Presentation is 12-15 minutes.	Presentation is 10 minutes.	Presentation is 8-9 minutes.	Presentation is less than 8 minutes.
Creativity	Presentation is unique and creative throughout.	Presentation is often unique and creative.	Presentation is average in creativity.	Presentation is boring and predictable.
Organization	Presentation is well organized and logical.	Presentation is organized and logical.	Presentation makes some sense.	Presentation is neither organized nor logical.
Complete Sentences	Complete sentences are used throughout.	Complete sentences are used about 75% of the time.	Complete sentences are used about 50% of the time.	Complete sentences are used less than 50% of the time.
Information Included	Thoroughly describes 10 items with several supporting facts about each.	Describes 10 items with many supporting facts about each.	Describes 10 items with a few supporting facts about each.	Lists 10 or fewer items with few supporting facts.

Index